# How to Make a Crafty Income

## A guide to selling at craft fairs and other events

### Brenda Hunt

Brenda Hunt

Copyright © Brenda Hunt 2013

All rights reserved world wide
No part of 'How to make a crafty income' may be reproduced or stored by any means without the express permission of Brenda Hunt

Whilst reasonable care is taken to ensure the accuracy of the information in this publication, no responsibility can be accepted for the consequences of any actions based on any opinions, information or advice found in the publication.

Any Business information contained in this publication should not be taken as a substitute for professional advice. It is your own responsibility to comply with all legal, accounting and tax regulations. Please seek advice from your legal and accounting advisors. The author and publisher of this book used their best efforts in producing this book and disclaim liability arising directly or indirectly from the use of the information in this book.

ISBN-13: 978-1490480466
ISBN-10: 1490480463

# CONTENTS

**INTRODUCTION** ...................................................7
**WHAT TYPE OF CRAFT?** ...................................13
    Easy to set up..................................................16
    Where to sell ...................................................18
    When to sell.....................................................19
    The benefits of selling face to face .....................20
    With an on-line presence. .................................22

**SETTING YOUR PRICES**....................................24
    Your Business Costs .........................................25
    The cost of One Unit ........................................26
    Parts ...............................................................27
    Packaging........................................................28
    % of fixed costs ...............................................29
    % of marketing costs........................................29
    Your time ........................................................30
    Setting your prices ..........................................30
    Your competitors price ....................................33
    What the market will stand...............................34

**WHAT'S YOUR STYLE?**.....................................36
    Focus your attention........................................37
    Who is your target customer.............................40
    Creating your brand ........................................40
    Designing your logo ........................................41
    Unique Selling Point.........................................44

## THE CRAFT FAIR .................................................. 46
- Finding your fair ................................................... 47
- What fair to choose ............................................. 48
- What the organiser expects from you. ................ 52
- Research ............................................................. 53
- The Fair overall .................................................. 54
- Your Craft ........................................................... 55
- Other Crafts ....................................................... 56

## SETTING UP YOUR CRAFT STAND ................... 59
- The Basics .......................................................... 62
- The Cover ........................................................... 62
- The Height ......................................................... 64
- Lighting ............................................................... 66
- Exhibition Banners ............................................ 68
- The rest of your equipment bag ........................ 68
- To show or not to show? ................................... 70

## MAKING A SALE .............................................. 72
- Setting your stall ................................................ 75
- Finishing off the sale in style ............................ 76
- The power of the impulse purchase .................. 77
- Making Valuable Contacts ................................. 79
- Personalised orders. .......................................... 82

## OTHER SELLING OPPORTUNITIES ................. 85
- School and church fairs. .................................... 85
- Country shows ................................................... 86
- Christmas markets. ............................................ 89
- Wedding fairs. .................................................... 90
- Home and furnishing shows .............................. 95

House parties .................................................96
Markets ........................................................100
Talks to social and church groups ......................101
Demonstrations .............................................104
Be prepared to expand......................................105

## HOW MUCH STOCK TO MAKE........................108

Creating your stock .........................................109
New designs....................................................110
Following fashion.............................................111
Storing your stock ...........................................112
Buying in Bulk. .................................................114

## HOW TO PROMOTE YOURSELF.....................116

Price promotions ............................................116
Bundled discounts...........................................117
Time specific discounts. ...................................118
Free gifts........................................................119
Sale time........................................................120
Product promotion. .........................................121
Talking about your craft. ..................................122
Demonstrating your craft.................................125
Seasonal promotions ......................................126
The Christmas season......................................128
The other side of Christmas..............................135

## RECORDING YOUR PROGRESS......................137

Keeping Score .................................................137
The Business of Business ..................................139
Find some expert advice ..................................139
Legal Requirements .........................................139

**Forms of Business Organisation** ........................**140**
        Sole Trader............................................140
        Partnership ............................................141
        Limited Company ..................................142
**What does this mean for you?** ..........................**143**
**The Tax Office** ....................................................**144**
**VAT**......................................................................**146**
**Other legal requirements** ..................................**148**
**Insurance** ...........................................................**149**

# GROWING YOUR BUSINESS. ..........................151

    **Where will you go from here**.............................**151**
    **Selling online.** ....................................................**153**
    **The future**..........................................................**154**

# Introduction

Crafting of any type is a great hobby, but there comes a point with any craft where you simply can't fit any more pictures on your walls, cushions on your sofas, rings on your fingers or have totally run out of people to give gifts to.

Crafting and choosing the handcrafted look is very fashionable at the moment, but not everyone has the time – or more importantly – the skills to create their own handcrafted items. Of course, this means that there is a market waiting to be filled and you are ideally positioned to fill it.

If you are reading this book, you are already crafting and have at least reached the stage of thinking about turning your hobby into a business, which is a very exciting – and sometimes scary – point to be at in your life. A bit like being at the edge of a cliff deciding whether to leap off with a big kite strapped to your back - terrifying but wonderful once you've made the leap!

Another, more serious reason to be thinking about turning your hobby into a business, is the state of the employment market at the moment. Many people now need or want to take control of their own lives, and even if you don't want to give up an existing job altogether, adding an independent income to the pot can help enormously in these financially difficult times.

Turning your hobby into a part time or even full time business can be the answer to many problems, but as in any business venture, it is best to be prepared before you take that leap into the unknown, and that is the whole purpose of this book.

In writing it, I have assumed a few things:

That you are good at your craft, you are producing items that are a high enough standard to ask someone to pay you for them.

That you want to run your own successful business but you're not aiming to supply all the big high street stores – not at the moment anyway!

And that you are interested in selling directly to your customer, face to face, at craft fairs and other events.

I have assumed that, although you want your business to be successful, you're not actually aiming to take over the world, become a household name and a multi-millionaire.

While they are perfectly good aims in life, they are not everyone's aim, and I have not written this book for those who want to start their business by investing thousands or even tens of thousands of pounds or dollars. I have written it for those of us who want to start on a shoestring, possibly combine a new craft business with an existing career and be comfortably successful.

In the past, if you wanted to sell your handcrafted goods you either had to sell them direct to your customer at craft fairs and other events or through someone else, for instance in a craft shop or a cafe.

Nowadays when you mention turning your hobby into a business, the first thing anyone thinks of it selling online - Etsy and Folksy, as well as many other specialist websites, your own website, ebay or amazon.

There's no doubt that the growth of the internet and the increasing number of sites that are available to the small business and craftworker, has changed the business model for many thousands of people and literally opened up the world – but it's not the whole answer.

There's still a place for selling face to face to your customer.

Some products don't really suit selling by mail – which is what selling on the internet still is. The internet might be a different way of reaching your customer - you don't have to print a fancy catalogue anymore, or do mail shots and place adverts in magazines and the newspapers – but you still have to actually ship your product once you've made a sale.

Some crafters don't want to use the internet for a number of different reasons. Some products don't really suit the process of selling by post – they might be very fragile, heavy but low cost or very bulky.

Some people don't feel comfortable with a computer, certainly not with the idea of running a business on line. They don't want the hassle of taking good quality photos and writing descriptions, they don't want to set up a website or maintain their listings on someone else's website – whether that is a small specialist site or one of the major players.

There is a lot of extra work involved in packing and posting, and it can become a very full time job, with customers expecting deliveries within days – if not sooner! Deciding to take your business on line can be very exciting, challenging and rewarding – but it won't suit everyone.

And of course, many craftworkers want to combine internet and face to face selling in their business.

So despite all the talk of the internet, there is still a place for selling face to face, even combining it with an on-line presence.

When you mention face to face selling, the automatic reaction is 'craft fairs' and that is certainly one type of event that you should consider, and the main focus of this book. They are a very good place to start, you can learn the skills you need and then branch out into other types of event.

I started selling at craft fairs almost twenty years ago when I had to find a new way of running a business.

I have been in business since the late 1970s (oh, that makes me feel old - I started very young!) And for many years I ran a business with lots of staff, dealing with big multinational companies, and lots of overseas interests, and I loved it. Marketing has always been one of my main interests and I studied business management at university and also mentored small and start up businesses and those wanting to enter the world of enterprise – I've always had a passion for helping people with some practical advice about getting started in business!

But things changed dramatically when I was diagnosed with M.E. (chronic fatigue syndrome). I had to make some rather drastic changes in my life. That is when I looked to my hobbies and decided to create a new, much smaller and easier to contain business that I could work on my own and around my new restricted circumstances.

Over the years I have concentrated first of all on creating a range of hand printed and painted cards and stationary and in more recent years, making gemstone jewellery, concentrating on the healing energies of the gemstones after discovered healing energy therapy for my own personal use and then studying various forms of alternative therapy.

I have run this much smaller business through craft fairs and other events and online websites. I can work from home and set my own timetable, and even though I would never have imagined I would be doing this, I love this lifestyle as well.

This is a type of business that you can create to suit your own requirements and work around your own lifestyle.

Once you start looking at craft fairs you will find that there are a huge range of events in this sector, from the small summer fair at the local church or school, to huge events lasting days in some of the major exhibition centres and at major events such as flower shows and country fairs at stately homes.

Craft fairs are often the first step in creating a new business and much of the information that you need for a business selling at craft fairs can then be adapted to other types of events, so I have concentrated on the craft fair model for this book.

But craft fairs aren't the only events on offer and once you've learnt the basics you can spread your wings.

The list of face to face opportunities can be quite extensive and some depend on your craft. Card making, jewellery and some types of hand sewn crafts can be adapted beautifully for wedding designs, which would mean that wedding fairs would be a good choice. While other crafts such as pottery, glass or soft furnishings would make a home design fair an excellent choice.

As you read this book, hopefully you'll be able to think of different ways that your range of handcrafted items can be made to appeal to different groups of customers and learn how to expand your fledgling business empire so that you can create a business that suits you and your lifestyle.

# What Type of Craft?

The type of craft business that you choose to set up obviously depends on your particular skills, but it can help to know the market before you decide which direction to take. For instance, if your skill lies in woodwork, should you concentrate on furniture, children's toys, decorative items such as shelving and frames, garden tubs, or nursery furniture?

The most popular crafts in the craft industry are textiles, ceramics, wood, glass, paper craft and jewellery.

But one of the benefits of choosing craft as a business is that you can adapt your skills quickly to take advantage of changing fashions. You don't have to go through committees, meetings and long product assessments - you can spot a trend and pounce!

There are a number of things to take into account before you decide what direction to take with your craft.

You might find that you have already made decisions without even realising it. Every skill can be turned to a number of different uses and you might have already have settled on one. For instance if you love knitting, you might already have impressed people with your talent for creating 'one off' pieces of wearable artwork, you might be well known for creating beautiful children's jackets or fantastic, imaginative shawls. But you might not have finalised your choices yet, in which case it's worth doing some market research before you spend weeks – or months – creating your stock for the first fairs.

Some crafts are already crowded with people creating in that area. In fact different crafts go in and out of fashion over the years, not so much in actually selling the finished product, but the actual craft itself. For instance knitting was incredibly popular in the 1980's, then hand knitting went completely out of fashion and all the wool shops closed down, now it is now popular enough again to have loads of magazines dedicated to it and some beautiful yarns available to work with.

When an actual craft is in fashion, lots of people will try it out, some will also try to sell their work even through some of them won't have reached a professional enough level. It's also true that some crafts always tend to attract a lot of people to them and if that is your area of work, you will have to make sure that your designs and products are different to the rest of the crowd.

For instance, you'll always find a lot of jewellery or handmade cards at fairs, but that doesn't mean that you can't carve out your own special niche and create a loyal band of clients who will follow you from fair to fair and recommend you to their friends. After all, look around your local high street or shopping mall, you'll certainly find quite a few places to buy jewellery or a greeting card and they all have customers, so seeing a lot of competition is not something to be scared of, you just have to create your own unique style.

So when you visit fairs to learn what your new market place will be like, you will probably see quite a number of stands selling jewellery or papercrafting – but that doesn't mean they'll all be the same.

Some will be selling very similar pieces, but unfortunately that probably means that the individual crafters won't be around for very long. People who buy handcrafted items do so because they want something different, something that sets them apart from the crowd, something that they can't just go and buy on the high street. So in order to be successful in the long term, you need to be able to offer your customers something that they can't get elsewhere.

Spend some time looking around, seeing what others create in your craft area – woodwork, knitting, jewellery, ceramics, chutneys – and adapt your skills to produce something different. After all, you want to make your mark with your new business not simply copy other people's ideas – a habit that would make you very unpopular as well! Craft fairs are very friendly, helpful places to work and craft workers are very generous with their help and advice, but no one like to have their ideas stolen.

You also have to take into account that you will spend a great deal of time working on your craft once it becomes your business, so it's very important to pick something that you will actually enjoy doing. Making a few cards for friends and family every month is a very different thing to making hundreds of cards every month and repeating the same design over and over to build up a stock of your best sellers.

No matter how much you love painting bright red poppies it can become a bit of a chore when you have to paint sixty of them on invitations for a special party order! So make sure that you choose something that you love doing, as well as something that you can see a market for.

You also need to remember that there is a difference between creating gifts for friends and selling to people you know, and taking that exciting step to actually running your own business.

You must make sure that your skills are of a high enough standard for you to be considered a professional craft worker.

The craft fair organisers will expect you to create to a high standard and so will your customers. The last thing you want is to have customers bringing your creations back to you because they've fallen apart.

Make sure that you have thought of all the stages of your craft and if there are any parts of the process that you are a little less confident with, work on it to improve your skill in that area.

You can find lots on help on-line or you could take a course or study it yourself through books, a course at your local craft shop or evening classes.

## Easy to set up

Many people dream of running their own small business, but many of them never take that step.

The process can seem overwhelming for many types of business, - finding premises, giving up your job, financing stock and equipment, specialist training - but many of the problems can be avoided when setting up a business selling at craft fairs.

The downfall of many small businesses can be summed up in one word - "overheads".

Many enterprises simply collapse under the weight of costs that they just can't support, especially in the beginning.

* The set up costs
* The equipment
* The stock
* The premises
* Employing staff
* Insurance
* And of course the dreaded cash flow problem of late payment.

Setting up your new business from a hobby and selling face to face at a range of different events can help you avoid most of the larger costs and problems of a business start up.

Set up costs will be very low, some display equipment, parts, some printing and rent for craft fairs.

You will already have a lot of the equipment because it has been your hobby.

Your premises will be a spare bedroom or the kitchen table, you might even be lucky enough to have a craft room.

You can keep a tight control of your stock levels, your staff is normally 'you' and in general you sell your products for cash, so late payment is not a problem either and although you do need insurance, you won't cost a fortune.

Craft businesses also have a relatively high success rate in comparison with other types of business, UK government figure show that more than 90% are still in business after 5 years, a survival rate that is more than three times that for the average small business.

Finally, it is very possible to start and even continue your craft business alongside your existing career. Most craft fairs take place at weekends and you can choose the time that suits you to actually make your stock, so you can try out your new business before burning your bridges and actually giving up a secure income!

Although there are a number of creative business that have been set up after or during University at craft fairs and have gone on to become successful businesses, there are also many crafters who have run their craft business alongside a full time job for many years, while for others it becomes a business once they retire.

## Where to sell

Selling in this way is a very direct business.

If you concentrate on Craft Fairs - which is the main type of business that this guide is aimed at - you take a stall and wait for the people to arrive. It is up to the organiser to get the people to the show and then up to you to sell to them.

Obviously some events are better than others and some events will suit you more than they will suit other crafts. You can only really discover this by trial and error and you will have a better feel for the type of event that is worth your investment in time and money when you look back at your figures for the first year.

Craft fairs and the larger events that include a craft marquee, are a popular day out and people tend to go to them with a different attitude than they have for a visit to a shopping centre.

They want to spend their money so much that often they pay to get in to see you. In return you have to offer them a product that they can't simply go to the shops and buy.

People that take the time to visit craft fairs are looking for something different, something creative that can complement their personality and very often, they are prepared to pay a premium price for the fact that you can create something unique.

## When to sell

Again, if you choose craft fairs it's really up to you. You can decide to simply attend a few fairs a year for some extra holiday money or you can travel the country making it a full time business and indeed, a way of life.

Many crafters travel throughout the country in their mobile homes or camper vans, setting up shop in a different show every weekend.

The type of business that you create is entirely up to you and this will help you decide what type of craft fair you choose and how far from home you decide to travel.

Craft fairs can be found almost throughout the year. Some organisers specialise in different times, such as pre-Christmas from September onwards, or the big summer events, but if you want to, you can create a full calendar.

For about five years, my show calendar started in the second or third week of January and continued every weekend until the week before Christmas – which was sometimes Christmas Eve! It's a little less hectic at the moment – after all I need some time to write!

So, a craft business is easy to set up, flexible enough to fit in with your life, even fitting in with your existing career. It is rewarding, has a high chance of success and while it probably won't make you fabulously wealthy, it will allow you to make you an income. It can be a full time career and it might possible give you a whole new lifestyle.

## The benefits of selling face to face

There are many reasons to choose this business model for your venture, whether you combine it with an on-line presence or not.

If you decide to just sell face to face you can have more control over when you will work. It might suit your family to have a business where you only work part of the year, you may choose to focus on Christmas crafts, spending most of the year building up your stock and then actually doing as many events as possible from September to December.

You may spend part of the year abroad and concentrate your selling at the time you're home, or if you have a young family or grandchildren you may choose to focus on events during term time leaving the holidays free.

Any of these patterns of work are possible when you sell at events, while they are very difficult if you sell online.

If you have your own website or sell through one of the big websites, it can easily become a seven day week and a 52-week year, with people expecting you to be available and to send out orders almost immediately.

Even if you close for a two week holiday you'll find yourself checking your emails daily so that any queries don't become problems before you can answer them!

This is fine if you are prepared for it and can manage that work pattern, but selling at craft fairs can be one of the most flexible and family friendly ways to run a business. You don't need to worry about what's happening while you're away and you can take time out from your business to manage your lifestyle.

Selling face-to-face also allows you to actually see how your designs are being received and to discuss what your customers are actually looking for.

When you are in the creative industry you need to be able to interact with people, both other creative people and your customers, so that you can keep your ideas fresh. It can be very difficult to keep coming up with new ideas and new designs if you spend your life in front of computer screens.

So there are many reasons to stick with the business model of selling face to face at craft fairs and other events. It may not be the latest most fashionable way of selling, but not everything has moved on-line, no matter what the media might make you think. If it had they wouldn't still be building supermarkets and shopping malls!

## With an on-line presence.

If you do sell on-line, you can use the craft events as both an advertising campaign and for your market research, as well actually getting the chance to interact with your customers and other crafters and of course – make sales.

Sitting in front of a computer can be quite an isolating experience and not the best way of stimulating your imagination!

When you are setting up your craft stall, make sure that you have plenty of promotional material for your website – give out cards and leaflets with your web address, set up special discount offers to direct customers to your website and to encourage them to buy again. Businesses – even very large business – often concentrate on attracting new customers, and while that is always very important, repeat customers and customer recommendation can be the bedrock of a successful business.

You can also get your customers to sign up for your e-mail list so that you can keep them up to date with your latest designs, special offers and of course a list of the events where they can find you.

You also need to make your on-line presence and your craft fair presence work together as two parts of a whole business.

Keep your style consistent. Use the same colour schemes and keep your logos the same on your websites and the paperwork at the fairs – and of course – use the same business name.

Make sure that your prices at the fair link up with the prices on your website.

While it's fine to have your event prices set lower than your on-line prices you should never do it in reverse. You can have special offers for the show 'on the day' to encourage people to make that impulse purchase. After all, from the point of view of your costs, you don't have to package and post the items if the customer buys from you there and then at the show, so you can afford to discount your prices.

But don't have your prices set higher at an event than in your on line shop. A customer will feel cheated if they have paid more at the fair than they see later when checking your website, and you will have lost a potential repeat customer.

Of course you can also use your website to advertise which events and shows you will be exhibiting at – although you should remember that if you trade from your home, you are also producing a list of times when your home will be empty! Personally I don't put a list of events on my websites, both because of the security concerns and the fact that my on-line customers are all over the world and my events list is very local.

If you are very social media savvy, you could link a blog to the website to keep customers up to date and make them feel part of a community.

You can also get them to fill in an information card to sign up for your e-mailing list and then keep them up to date on what is happening in your business.

# Setting your Prices

The whole point of being in business - any business, no matter how large or small - is to make money.

That might not be a popular idea with everyone, it might smack of capitalism and big business, but it's fact. Even if you are just funding your hobby you have to make money, otherwise you won't be able to buy the parts to make any more stock.

At the end of the day, you have to make money!

That is also the whole reason for running a charity or fund raising event – you have to actually be left with some money for the good cause at the end of everything.

So whatever way you look at it, and whatever your reasons - money is your final objective - along with enjoying yourself of course.

The method of reaching this important goal is to get your costing right, a process that many people find very difficult.

Many craft workers have a tendency to undersell themselves. Lack of confidence in yourself or your work is a serious problem for many people setting up a craft business and it leads to a tendency to undercharge for work. Obviously you have to price your designs to sell, but you also have to make money!

In order to work out how much you are going to charge for your product you have to take three main points into account.

Your business costs
Your competitor's prices
What the market will stand

## Your Business Costs

Businesses have two types of cost - *Fixed* and *Variable*

Fixed costs are those which are not affected directly by the amount you sell. Items such as rent, rates, the wages of permanent staff, lease payments for equipment.

These costs - the overheads - do not alter unless your turnover changes significantly. For instance, if your orders increase so much that you need bigger premises.

If you have a specific amount in mind that you wish to draw from your business as a wage, this is a fixed cost and should be calculated in at the time. And don't forget insurance cover!

Variable costs are those which are affected directly by the number of units of your product that you make.

Raw materials

packaging

electricity for running machines or heating your workshop area

overtime pay or piecework rates if you have staff – although you staff normally consists of you and other members of your family!

Fixed costs have to be built into your price structure at the beginning. For instance, if you sell 1000 units a year, 1000th of your fixed cost has to be included in the overall cost of each unit. If you don't do this you will be steadily making a loss each time you make a sale.

Fixed costs also determine the number of units you have to sell in a year to reach a break even figure. If your overheads are £5,000 a year and you calculate that you can include £5 for overheads in the price of each unit, you have to sell 1,000 units over the year to break even - after that you start to make a profit. However, if you can only include .50p in the price of each unit, you will have to sell 10,000 units to avoid making a loss.

## The cost of One Unit

To find your business costs you need to know exactly how much each design costs you to produce.

Parts
Packaging
% of fixed cost
% of marketing

Your Time - a very important item that most small business people neglect!

One of the benefits of running a small business such as a craft business, is that the fixed costs or overheads can be kept very low. Most of your costs are directly related to the product you produce. You probably don't need special premises, most craft businesses can be run from home, you probably won't need any staff and equipment can be kept to a minimum.

## Parts

Each unit you make takes a certain amount of raw material or parts. Work out exactly how much each product costs.

How much fabric do you use for each cushion - ¼ meter, ½ meter, 2 meters of trim?

How many glasses can you paint from each pot of paint - 1, 15, 42?

How many balls of wool does it take to knit each toy or jumper?

How many beads do you use for each necklace?

Look at each of the products you intend to make and work out exactly what is in each of them and how much it will cost.

Another very important thing about your parts cost is how much you actually pay your supplier.

When you are making a small number of presents as a hobby, you probably buy your raw materials in the local craft shop. But when you are thinking of expanding this hobby into a business, it's time to really think about how much you are spending, and how you can reduce it.

Look around for wholesalers, ask what the reduction will be for bulk purchases, see if there are any factory or mill shops selling what you need, read the adverts in the craft magazines and send for price lists, asking for their wholesale prices.

Of course, buying in bulk will mean that you have to spend more money initially and that you will be holding stock - which can take up a lot of space for some crafts - but it can also mean a drastic reduction in unit costs.

Work out how much you will save on each item, how much you will need to invest in stock and then decide if the saving is worth the initial outlay. It can vary for different crafts, but as a general rule, once you start creating your designs as a business you should look at purchasing your parts from a wholesale supplier.

## Packaging

Working out the cost of packaging is very similar to working out the cost of parts.

In order to look professional, and give your potential customer confidence in your product, you have to package it - mount it on a card, put it in a box, protect it if it's fragile, put a label on it, put it in a bag – every product needs some form of packaging.

In the past I have worked with two different crafters who both produced beautiful decorative objects. The work was lovely, pieces from either of them made beautiful gifts but they had very different attitudes to packaging. One of them had a pile of creased old newspapers and used carrier bags from all the local supermarkets, and each purchase of their wonderful work was unceremoniously stuffed in an old bag!. The other had lovely tissue paper, simple white boxes with her trade name and details on a label and she finished off each box with some lovely floristry ribbon and a flourish! Guess who used to have a queue at her stall?

Packaging can make all the difference.

Whatever you decide is needed, it has to be paid for. As some supermarkets tell you, there's no such thing as a free carrier bag!

Find a supplier who can provide a bulk quantity and work out how much each bag will cost. If a bag is .01p you have to add that to your cost, likewise, if a box is £2 you have to include that amount in your calculation.

You may also be able to make the packaging - or at least enhance it - yourself. Look into this, but remember that your time is money and it could be cheaper in the long run to buy packaging readymade and just add a label, concentrating your time on your actual product.

## % of fixed costs

Make a judgement as to how many units you think you will sell (at first this has to be a guess - you won't be able to make a real judgement until you have done your first few craft fairs) and divide your fixed costs by that number.

## % of marketing costs

Marketing is the amount you might spend on producing stationary, leaflets, cards, or on advertising.

The actual cost of each craft fair - either the stand or the cost of the stand and the expenses of being there if you are away from home - can be dealt with as either a marketing or fixed cost for this type of business. Strictly it should be a variable cost as it varies with how many units you sell, but when you are selling through craft fairs it takes the place of your permanent premises and the rent and rates your would pay for that.

## Your time

This is a very important element and one that a great number of people simply neglect to consider - the argument being that you're not doing anything else with that time anyway, so anything you get is better than nothing.

But that isn't the point. You could do something else with your time, something more profitable - or you could choose to concentrate on more profitable items in your range.

Time how long it takes you to make one unit of each of your chosen products from start to finish. If one type of toy takes 15 minutes and one takes 45 minutes, each uses the same amount of materials, is sold at the same price and they sell as well as each other - then you should concentrate on the one that takes you the least time, because you can make three of the first or only one of the second in the same time - which means that the first pays you three times as much for your time. You should also work out how you can simplify the second design to bring the time down.

## Setting your prices

Setting your prices is one of the most important parts of your business and can quickly lead to failure if you get it wrong. Too low and you will lose money, no matter how much you sell. Too high and you won't sell anything!

So how do you decide?

Now that you have worked out your costs, you know exactly how much each design costs you to make.

You know how much the packaging will cost for it and how much of your fixed costs you should include on each piece.

You also have to take the market into account when setting your prices.

How much do other people charge? If your product is twice the price of any close alternative it probably won't sell! Of course there may be a reason for the price difference. Your jewellery may be gold while others are silver, or it might be sterling silver where the others are silver plated. But if your product is basically the same, your prices also have to be in line with the market.

It's obvious to everyone that you can set your prices too high, but you can also set them too low.

Many people go into business thinking that they have to undercut their competitors. In fact it's become one of the main lines of advertising in many industries – 'we're the cheapest' 'save money by coming to us' 'we'll undercut any genuine quote' – they can't all be the cheapest!

But for small businesses this can be a real disaster if you choose it as your main sales method.

The fact is, that you can never be the cheapest because someone will come along and undercut you – even if that does mean that they are losing money on every sale. Your designs are handcrafted, unique, and individual – respect yourself!

The fact is, that being cheap doesn't create the impression you want with your potential customer.

If something is much cheaper than the alternatives, the natural reaction is to think that it is not as good, that it is flawed in some way, a cheap copy. Is that the image you want to create for your work?

So, work out how much each item will cost you to make, how much it will cost you to sell, what the general price range should be and finally what you feel you can charge.

I have seen earrings that are basically exactly the same – sterling silver hooks, amethyst gemstone 8mm beads – the same basic design, the same size, made with the same skill – but sold at a vast range of prices. I've seen some people display them as fine jewellery, pack them beautifully in jewellery boxes, and sell them at £70 as designer gemstone jewellery. I've also seen others just lie them flat on the table among dozens of other pieces, put them in a paper bag and sell them from less than £5 as if they were silver plated and glass beads.

Each type of fair, each part of the country, even different times of the year will have different selling experiences for you at first. Find your own middle ground for your own product and work from there.

You may find that your competition is other craft sellers at the fair, but for other products it might be that your competition is the high street, designer stores or specialist home decor stores.

Each business is different and one of the real benefits of selling at craft fairs is that you can experiment with different prices at different fairs and events until you know what is right for you.

## **Your competitors price**

When you are doing your initial research at craft fairs, one of the things you will check are the prices your direct competitors are charging. As I say, that might be at the fairs or it might be specialist websites, departments stores or designer furniture stores.

Most crafters have competition in the craft fair world.

Within a single fair you will probably find that the prices between the stands for a particular type of craft are broadly similar. Between different fairs you may find a greater range of prices.

One of the great things about selling through craft fairs is that you can adapt your prices directly to the sales event, an option that a shop does not have.

Once you have a guide line on your competitors prices, you have found a benchmark for setting your own and as a rough guide you should aim to keep within a fairly tight band. If all the other jewellers are selling silver earrings for around £10 that's the price range that you should choose if your designs fall into the same general market.

Setting your own price too far below others is probably counter-productive. It will simply make your product look `cheap' rather than good value for money and if you do make sales you could simply be throwing the extra money away as well as upsetting your fellow crafters.

Setting your prices too high will probably mean that you lose sales - unless your product is clearly of higher quality, for instance it's gold rather than silver, silk rather than cotton, fine china rather than pottery.

## What the market will stand

In all areas of business, this is the real trick to setting your prices. A four bedroom detached house in one area of the country might be built to exactly the same design as that in another area but be valued at double the price, and two shirts may be almost identical but if one has a designer label it will sell for a much higher price than the supermarket one.

As you have already seen, craft fairs are no different in this respect to any other form of business. Prices do vary between different events and it is an odd but true fact that an identical item offered by the same crafter will sell for two or three times the price at one craft fair rather than another, especially if the events are very different and in different parts of the country.

One way to judge this is to keep a record of the prices you see others charging when you do your research, another is to try it out for yourself.

This is the kind of price differential that can make it well worthwhile to invest in the large, more expensive events. The increase that you can get in your product price is almost pure profit once you have sold enough units to cover the additional cost of being at the fair.

The image of your product can also increase the price you can charge. Take a look at the more up-market stores or at the adverts in the quality magazines. The actual product is often very similar basically to a lower cost product, but the detailing of the product itself and the quality of the packaging puts it into a different league, a much higher value league.

The fact that your product is hand crafted (handmade not homemade) automatically puts it into a quality band, so it could be well worth while to spend some time on creating a more intricate design, a more unique slant on your craft or a smarter more expensive form of packaging.

Variations in craft fairs enable you to experiment with your prices and the overall image of your product.

Alter the prices at each fair at first to see what affect it has on your total sales and remember, it's not only the number of units that you sell that matters, it's the total profit that you make. Selling 100 units at a low price could earn you less than selling 30 at a higher price, and at the end of the day, the thing that matters is the amount of profit you have made.

One final item that you should take into account when setting your prices is the shelf life of your product.

If it is very perishable - sweets, jam, plants for instance - you may wish to accept a lower unit price and lower wastage. On the other hand, if your product has a long shelf life you can afford to take it home with you again and put it back into stock until you find the right person willing to pay you what it is worth.

# What's your style?

You probably haven't thought about your style before.

You just make your craft for your own pleasure, probably as gifts for friends and family, maybe even for orders from friends and work colleagues. Most small handcrafted businesses start off like this, almost by accident.

But all along you will have been developing a style, even if it's not well-defined yet.

Now is the time to think seriously about it.

When you decide to take the step to selling your handcrafted designs, which you have or are about to if you're reading this book, you need to start developing a style of your own.

No business, no matter how large it is, can be all things to all people, and when you're a small business that is even more true.

So rather than trying to do everything and attract every conceivable type of customer, concentrate on one thing, aimed at one type of customer and do it really well.

## Focus your attention

There are many interpretations of style in any craft.

For the case of this argument, think about handcrafted jewellery.

When I say you should concentrate on one thing and do it really well, I don't mean that you should only make Amethyst jewellery, or one design of gemstone earrings, although that could work. After all, what comes to mind when you think of the brand Pandora? You think of bracelets and charms, even though they do make other styles of jewellery. That could seem rather limited, but Pandora doesn't seem to have been at all limited by it.

You can find other examples of big brands, some of which specialise in designs that are quite simple, gemstone bead stretch bracelets or bead necklaces, but that hasn't stopped them becoming large, well-known brands.

So, look at the craft items that you make and decide what the main elements are.

Again sticking with jewellery for the sake of this, do you work with precious metals, copper, sterling silver or gold vermeil and 9ct gold? Or do you work with silver plated and gold plated parts? Maybe your main designs are done with bead stringing, bead weaving, macramé or wire work.

Do you work with gemstones - if so are they beads, cabochon or faceted gemstones? How do you use them, do you string them or set cabochons into precious metal cast settings.

Do you work with acrylic beads, glass, exclusive Murano glass, wooden or clay beads? Or are your designs quirky, based on old buttons or other vintage pieces? Do you make your own glass pendants, polymer clay beads or do you focus on recycling in your art?

Do you make dainty pendants or chunky bead necklaces? Do you work with subtle colours or a riot of brights or perhaps you prefer a palette of blacks!

You could go through a similar process for most crafts.

If you work with wood, are the pieces of wood you choose special and rare, do you create hand turned bowls, fountain pens, quirky ornaments, useful kitchen or office pieces, large pieces of furniture, traditional designs for children, garden furniture? Do you hand paint your pieces with traditional flower designs, or colour them with bright primary colours, include a unique handcarved design into each piece as your special signature, or carve intricate swags and tails that are finished with gold leaf?

Every craft has a huge range within it and you can use your skills to create something that is unique to you – creating your own style. In fact, once you start to think about it, you'll find that you do actually have a style of your own, a style that you can develop and become known for.

When you've decided on your main style and what you feel you want to concentrate on, you can begin to make decisions about what you think your design and image should be.

At this stage it's probably worth discarding some of the designs that really don't fit into your new design style.

As we decided earlier, you can't be all things to all people, so now is the time to think about who your target customer is.

If your range is going to be fun and funky, aimed at the young and fashionably young at heart, you'd be wasting your time and investment by adding in a few traditional standard designs. Worse, you'd be diluting your image, confusing potential customers and alienating both sets.

Think about a fashion shop.

If you were looking in the window of a smart, classic, designer store aiming at the professional business woman, you probably wouldn't expect to see leopard print leggings in the window. If you were looking at a fun and funky boutique you wouldn't expect to see a traditional pastel Mother of the Bride outfit. Either one would be confusing and would undermine your confidence in the shop.

So it's best to drop the items that lie far outside your central style. They will just confuse your image and damage the overall look of your stand, making it look cluttered and unfocused.

Concentrate on creating a whole collection of designs that will look like they come from the same designer rather than having a mix and not match approach that will end up looking home-made rather than handmade.

## Who is your target customer

The best way of creating this collection is the way that big marketing companies go about it.

Decide who is your target customer is and design for him or her.

You build up a picture of the person you think will be buying your handcrafted items. What sort of age might she be? Which big name shops would she be buying in? Will she be keeping up with the latest trends or going for the classics? Will she be buying for her children as well as herself?

You don't want to be too rigid. After all you do want to sell as much as possible, but it does help focus your mind if you have a target customer to think about as you're planning.

## Creating your brand

Your image doesn't finish with your designs.

When you are designing and deciding on your target customer, think about how you will present your designs.

What name will you give your new collection? People love brands, and you have to decide on a name that you will put on your business cards and your leaflets. It can be your own name or an adaptation of your name or something completely different.

For instance, someone called Sarah Jane could call her new handmade handbag business Sarah Jane Handbags, Sarah Jane Designs, SJ Bags, SJ Handpainted Handbags. She could pick something entirely different. 'Bags of Bags',' Glitz & Glamour', 'Hand Candy'.

A brand name gives your customers something to follow. If they see a list of exhibitors at a craft fair, they will know whether you will be there. They'll be able to tell their friends who to look for. It's much better if they can say, look for 'Glitz & Glamour', rather than the tall girl with dark hair!

## Designing your logo

Now that you've got this far, you have your style and a business name, you can begin to think about the image of your entire business.

What will your colour scheme be? What sort of font will you use for your new business name? This is the point at which your business name becomes your logo.

Writing exactly the same word in a number of different fonts and using different colours will create different images.

Try this out on your computer.

Pick a simple name and repeat it a number of times on the page. Then use a different style of font each time – some heavy and blocky, some script, some with flourishes, some simple and rounded.

Once you print it out, you will see what a difference the different fonts can make. Again learn from the professionals - they spend millions of pounds making slight alterations to their logos. It might seem a terrible waste of money, but the way a brand is written affects the way we see them, and how we think of their services or their products.

Walk down the high street, through a shopping mall or flick through a glossy magazine. As an exercise, just look at the names of the businesses above the shop, on the windows or in the adverts. Look at the labels on produces and the style of the packaging. Don't look at the actual products for the moment, just at the style of the lettering. What font they have used for the company name and what colours they use to create their image. See what impression you get of their style and product just from this initial glance.

A simple name above a clothes shop can give a whole range of different images, due totally to the way that name is written and the colours that are used. The same word in different fonts and colours can give the impression of a shop aimed at children or babies, teenagers, the career woman or a glamorous granny. It can make it look up to date and funky, friendly, very up-market or cheap and cheerful. It can make it look exciting and on trend or dated and uninteresting. See what impressions you get from the name and style and then see if it matches the stock inside the shop.

The large stores seen in every town across the country will display the image they what you to see, but some of the independent shops will be more of a surprise! You can learn a lot by seeing what other people have done – right and wrong!

If you call your jewellery business Bridal Creations and use the style of traditional script font that is often used for bridal businesses, will give the impression of being traditional and elegant. Pictures of pearl tiaras and sparkling Austrian crystal necklaces will spring to mind as soon as someone reads your name.

But if you want to attract the more funky brides to your funky jewellery, then you want to choose a font and a style that will show them that you have something different to offer right from the very start.

And that start begins with your logo. It creates your image as soon as someone reads your name.

Branding is incredibly important, because unfortunately we really do judge a book by its cover and you only have a few seconds to catch the attention of a potential customer.

Now you're really beginning to get somewhere.

You know what kind of handcrafted pieces you're going to design and who you're going to sell it to. And you know what your company image looks like now that you've developed your business name and your logo.

You're beginning to feel like a real business.

None of these things have to cost you a fortune or even take that long to create, but it makes the difference between selling some home-made pieces at a church fete and selling your unique handmade designs at craft fairs and other events.

If you want to be taken seriously you have to look as if you are serious about running your business.

Having formed this idea of your style, you will find it easier to make other decisions about your new business.

Deciding what your colour scheme is. What colour covers you will have for your table. What type of packaging you will choose, what type of promotions you will run. It will even help focus your mind so that you can decide where you will sell your handmade designs.

## Unique Selling Point

Otherwise known as your USP, every business should have a unique selling point, but what is it!

It's what sets you, your business and your craft apart from other people. It's what your business stands for. It's what's important to you. It is also back to the point of not trying to be everything to everyone.

Working out what your USP is can help you focus your mind on what you actually want to do and how you want to be seen.

Okay, at its simplest, you want to sell your handmade designs.

But why do you want to make your product? Is one of your aims to get away from the mass production that we see nowadays? Do you love creating something totally unique, each piece you create a part of your own personality?

Do you want each of your intricate bead work patterns to be a unique work of art? Do you want to create something collectable, something that is valued as a piece of artwork as much as a piece of jewellery?

Do you concentrate on ethical sourcing of your wood for your hand carvings, or do you focus on recycling in your design work?

Take some time about your USP. It's a worthwhile process personally as well as for your business. It means that you will be concentrating on why you have started selling your hand crafted designs.

What do you love about the craft?

What do you love about the materials that you use?

What are your passions?

After all, this is not just a job. You have taken the decision to start a creative business of your own, and it's very exciting!

If it's not exciting, it might be time to rethink your plans, because it takes quite a lot of work to create a successful business from your love of craft, and you'll probably find yourself working and creating items late into the night sometimes in order to be ready for the next event – or even during events!

So it definitely needs to be something that you love doing. And that is the best part about this whole process - being able to make money from something you love doing. It means that you never really go to work!

# The Craft Fair

The main subject for this book is the Craft Fair, but many there are many other events that follow a similar style and we'll have a look at them in more detail later.

Even in the craft fair section, there are many different types and styles of event.

Some are going to be in your local area while others will involve long journeys.

Some last a few hours, some will take place over a few days or even a week and will involve you staying away from home.

The costs of fairs can vary enormously and so will the standards that are required of the crafter. A small, regular event in a market hall will have a totally different set of rules, costs and craft standards to a specialist craft association event at a large show.

You probably already visit craft shows – most crafters are interested in other crafts. So you are probably already familiar with some of your local regular shows and the larger events in your region.

A few searches on-line will give you lists of other organisers and events. Your local newspaper will carry adverts, tourist information offices will have leaflets and there will be adverts in their 'whats on' sections. When you are visiting fairs, some of the crafters will have lists of other events where they will be exhibiting. Gather all this information and file it away for future reference.

Over time you will also learn about other events, organisers will approach you as you work at fairs and they'll pick up your leaflets and cards so that they can telephone you about their school fairs and charity events. It won't take too long before you have to make decisions about which even you will book for certain weekends.

Most craftworkers start by showing at smaller, local fairs so that they can build up their experience and knowledge before tackling the larger more expensive events.

## Finding your fair

It can be totally bewildering to start with. How do you find craft fair organisers? There is a huge choice and it varies from the local church setting up a fair once or twice a year, to large companies who organise huge events around the country.

The charge varies dramatically as well, from about £30 a day for small local fairs to well into the high hundreds and more for four and five days at a large event.

Obviously you need to do more homework!

When you are doing your original research, try and find out who organised the fairs you visited. You will normally find someone at the door taking entrance fees, there may be some paperwork for you to pick up, normally a list of their other events - or just ask.

Most craft people are very friendly and they'll gladly tell you how to contact the organiser and how much you can expect to pay, and the organisers will certainly be interested in giving you information, after all you are their potential customer.

Local papers are also a good source of information. Organisers often advertise for stall holders in the classified section of the paper or advertise their event to the public. After all, their job is to get the people to the fair.

Check out the tourist information office and the local library for lists of what's on in your region. Again this will list craft fairs and big events such as country fairs and local events that will include a craft fair or craft tent. If the actual organiser is not named, a telephone call to the location will soon provide you with the information you need.

Look for magazines of local interest. Some are printed as holiday guides, some as community information. Again, they will list events for the region.

And of course the Internet is an excellent source of information.

## What fair to choose

When you look around, the choice of fairs can be almost too much. Where do you start?

At first it's probably best to remain fairly close to home until you get used to the whole business of doing craft fairs and gradually work your way up to the larger, longer and more expensive events.

Many of the larger events will not be open to you at first - you have to prove your expertise - but this is not a bad thing. You need to learn your trade, make your mistakes (hopefully not many after reading this!) and work your way up though the craft fair world before you make big investments in the large, prestigious events.

When you work out your costs you must calculate not only the actual stand cost, but the whole cost of getting to and being at an event.

How will you get you and your product to the fair? Will you drive? Will someone else drive you? Does that mean taking time off work?

How much fuel will it take?

Is your normal transport capable of travelling further distances or do you have to hire a car or van?

Will you need to join a recovery service such as the AA or RAC?

Will you need to change your car insurance to cover business use - you will if you intend to be on the road almost every weekend from fair to fair.

What amount of money do you need to allow for expenses - food on the road, food at the fair - for both yourself and whoever travels with you.

If the event is two or more days - where will you stay? Will you take a caravan, tent or campervan with you, or will you have to stay in a motel or bed & breakfast?

The whole choice of fair also depends on your own experience of travelling. Is 50 miles a long journey to you, or are you used to commuting that distance every day?

If it is a two or three day fair, can you travel to and from it each day or will you have to stay overnight?

How many fairs do you want to do each year?

If you intend your new venture to be a full time business rather than a part time extra, you will want to have as many sales opportunities as possible.

There are many full time crafters who travel around the country with their own self contained world in a caravan or campervan, to set up shop week after week at a different fair for a new set of customers.

These longer, larger craft events are often found at stately homes, at the big flower shows, country fairs, horse shows and all sorts of other large events and in the main tourist areas of the country, where thousands of people will arrive ready to spend their money at the show – hopefully some of it in the craft tent and some of that with you.

But you need a lot of capital to invest at the beginning of the season. The fairs have to be booked up months in advance, the booking charges for these events are at the higher end of the scale, your travelling expenses can be significant and you have to have a large amount of stock available to sell to make the investment in time and money worthwhile.

You might also need to invest in an actual stand. Most local craft fairs provide you with a table for your stand – most are the standard 6ft table and you can book 6ft or 12ft of space, but at larger events you are often booking the space – it can come in the form of an exhibition booth (three canvas walls) or just the actual floor space and you will have to supply your own tables and chairs. As the events become more 'professional' (read large and expensive) you will also have to pay for other things such as an electrical supply, your name above the space, you might even have to hire your electrical fittings and furniture through their exhibition supplier – it can become quite a large investment so you need to feel confident that you can sell enough of your product to still make a profit.

If you start with the smaller, local fairs it is much easier to set up your new business.

Again you do have to book up in advance - often many months in advance for the good fairs that are well attended - but the fees are much lower and you don't have to invest in so much stock.

The added advantage is that you can judge which items are selling and which are not and then adjust your stock accordingly without having to accept a big loss.

Local fairs are also the type of event when you will be more likely to make contacts about other local events, making it easier to expand your calendar.

Of course, some of the larger fairs will be in your own area - and in that case, for a few weekends a year - you can have the best of both worlds. The cost of a major fair may seem like a lot, but it can certainly be worthwhile. Many thousands of people attend a large event, as opposed to hundreds for a small craft fair. And they are more prepared to make purchases - after all the entrance fees for the general public are much higher at a large craft fair, and there's no point paying £6 or £7 or even £15 or £20 entrance if you have no intention of buying anything.

## What the organiser expects from you.

Most organisers insist that your product is hand crafted rather than bought in for the event and of course that is exactly what you want. This ensures a genuine craft fair rather than simply a market.

Within that broad description there are more specific requirements from some organisers.

There are some events that are aimed at the very highest level of the craft profession - graduates, students from art school, or those self taught crafters who have managed to achieve a high level of excellence. They are very difficult to get into and often require as high a level of self marketing skills as crafting skills. Some of these fairs are restricted to the members of a specific craft association, guild or society.

Most craft events are aimed at a more normal level but the organisers can still have high standards and it is in the interest of all crafters that they maintain the standards of their events to keep the confidence of the customers visiting the craft fair.

The larger organisers will insist that you have hand crafted the product yourself and will often encourage you to demonstrate your craft on the stand. Some will even supply additional stand space free of charge if you will be demonstrating.

They will want to see photographs or samples of your work and possibly photographs of your stand set up before accepting your booking.

Smaller, more local fairs are often less strict in their requirements. It's a good idea to use these events to work out the best way for you to display your product and set up your stand, and to build up a portfolio of photographs to send to those organisers that require them.

Although you should always have insurance to cover yourself - public liability at least - some of the larger organisers do demand a higher level of cover which also has to be taken into account in your costs.

There has been a growing trend for some organisers to hold craft and gift fairs, where you will be competing with products that are simply bought in. I find that these fairs can be a bit mixed. They can work and it does mean that you can add to your stock by buying in some readymade pieces, but the public can't always tell what you have made and what has been mass produced in China to look handmade. Of course, if it's been 'handmade' in China it will cost much less than your handcrafted designs. Personally I prefer to stay with pure craft fairs.

## Research

As with any business project, market research at the very beginning of your planning is vital to your success.

Once you decide to turn your hobby into a craft business you have to take other people and their tastes into account rather than just your own.

Your own personal style is obviously very important in making your craft unique, but it must be balanced with the need to actually sell your product to others.

But you'll be pleased to find that market research in this particular industry can be great fun. It involves visiting as many craft fairs as you can find, large and small. But instead of just browsing you must now really look at everything. Remember you are no longer simply a customer, you are a potential craft seller and you want to learn everything you can about your new business field.

Take notes while you are looking and then write them up for yourself when you get home. But remember these notes are about the craft fair, you are not copying somebody else's product. If you start stealing someone else's ideas not only is it immoral and will make you very unpopular, it will also mean that you have no style of your own.

You might find it useful to make yourself a report form with these questions;

## The Fair overall

Where is the fair being held - a church hall, a hotel, a leisure centre, a marquee?

Was it advertised - if so where? The local free papers, tourist information office, regional papers, local radio?

Was it signposted - outside the building, in the town on road signs, lamp posts, outside the town leading visitors into it?

Was it easy to find, where there clear directions?

Was there are entrance fee? How much was it, was it easy to get in or did you have to queue?

Was it a large fair - in more than one hall or marquee?

Was there a directory or list of exhibitors. If there was did you have to buy it or was it free?

How comfortable was the site. Was it cold or too hot, was it bright or too dark to see properly?

Were there any refreshment arrangements, any toilets, any facilities to encourage you to stay a while?

Was there enough space for each stallholder or was it so cramped that you felt you couldn't stop to look?

Did it feel friendly?

Were lots of people looking and buying, or was it very quiet?

Did it make you want to spend your money?

Was there a lot of choice or were half the stalls selling the same things?

Was the quality of the products on offer good? Were they hand crafted or were too many of the items mass manufactured or of a poor standard?

## Your Craft

Obviously you have to set up with a craft you are already familiar with. There's no point deciding to make children's clothes if you've never used a sewing machine in your life and some areas of craft have very specialist skills, such as the creating of collectable teddy bears, where you may well choose only to exhibit at teddy bear fairs.

On the whole, you do have to take note of what else is already on sale in your field and possibly adapt your skill to something slightly different. There's really no point in competing directly with other people. It will make you very unpopular, it could damage the sales of the established crafter and it won't create a unique image for your own work.

It's also worth while knowing what is in fashion - you can keep up to date with the latest colours or styles much more easily than a large manufacturer and it could give you the edge over other sellers at a craft event.

So the second part of your research at the fair is to check out the actual crafts on offer.

The main things you have to research about your craft area are:

How many competitors do you find at each fair you visit - at a good fair you should not find too many stands for each craft.

How similar are their products to each other and to your own - does each stand look the same or can you find real choice between the different crafters?

What are their prices - is there much variation?

How do they display the product, what does the stand look like, what colour schemes do they use?

Does the product seem popular with the public?

How do they package the product?

## Other Crafts

What range of other crafts and products do you find as you look around the fair? You should be able to find a good choice of different items.

Woodwork, paintings, photography, children's clothes, hand blown glass, ceramics, jewellery, papercraft, jams and chutneys, toys, dolls, teddy bears, silk flowers, cakes, jewellery boxes, pens, silk scarves, soaps and lotions, home decor – you get the idea. There should be plenty of choice. If you were doing your

Christmas shopping, you should be able to find gifts for everyone at a good craft fair.

After all, if you choose to book with that particular organiser, you don't want to find that almost every other stand is competing directly with you.

Is the quality of work good or does it look amateurish? You will find fairs that are pitched both too high and too low for your skills.

What sort of range do the overall prices fall into? Some events can be very high end while others seem to be trying to compete with a car boot or garage sale.

Within each craft, are they producing items that look interesting or are they all very basic?

Are there large pieces of work or do they mainly fall into the small, impulse buy bracket?

Once you have visited a few different craft fairs you should be able to build up a picture of the market available to you. Make sure that you research different types of fair, small local fairs, big events such as country shows with craft tents and the large specialist craft fairs.

When you have built up a clear picture of the full range available, you will be able to make some decisions on the type of product you will concentrate on, where and how you will offer it for sale and how much you will charge for it.

Do not be tempted to skip this part of the business process. Knowing your market is vital to the potential success or failure of your business enterprise and jumping in feet first is the easiest way to fail. It is very tempting to rush ahead a book you first fairs within weeks of having the idea, but it is also terribly disappointing as well as expensive to find yourself at that fair with the wrong product at the wrong price.

Making the wrong decisions about where to sell, can kill your plan to run your own craft business.

If you have jumped in and your first events are a disappointment, don't give up. Do some research and find the right places for you to start selling.

# Setting up your craft stand

When you actually book a craft fair, do check exactly what you will be supplied with. Is it simply the space? Will you have to take your own table and chairs or are they supplied? Do check, don't just assume.

You want to know exactly what you will be supplied with when you make your reservation. Some organisers - not many - supply simply the space, you will have to take your own table and chairs.

Others supply a table only if you book one specifically. So do check the details. The last thing you want to do is arrive early one morning and find you have nothing to set your stall out on or nowhere to sit for the entire day.

Most craft fair organisers supply a table and two chairs, but it's then up to you to turn a very basic, often tatty table into an attractive stand.

The standard table is 6ft long x 2ft wide and is often a trestle table. You normally have space behind the table for you to stand in and to put your chairs. You also normally have some space to the side, or both sides, between you and the next stand – but you don't always have this space, so don't rely on it. You can turn up first thing in the morning and find that all the stalls are in a single, solid line!

The space between the tables is to allow you and your neighbour to enter and leave your stand easily, to allow you to step from behind your stand and talk to a customer or replenish your display. Don't fill it with an extra stand or rail, or push your chair in front to use as more display space. Space invaders cause bad feeling and you'll find that other crafters no longer want to be quite so helpful. Crafters are normally very helpful to each other and you'll need the support – especially if you are on your own. Neighbours normally cover each other's stands so that you can get a coffee or take a quick break.

Some organisers will provide you with extra space free of charge if you will demonstrate your craft and this can be well worth doing - showing how to make something always seems to draw a crowd. But you will definitely need to have someone else with you to make sales while you are busy demonstrating

The table is your shop window and you only have a few seconds to catch the attention of the passing crowd. So you must make a good first impression. Make your public take that all important second look.

You may find yourself using tables from hotel dining rooms, factory canteens or, as I said earlier, they are very often trestle tables.

As a guide, a standard table will be about 6ft long by 2ft wide, and remember -you have to carry and put up the rest of your stand yourself, so you need something that looks good without taking a small lorry to transport it and an hour to put together.

As I said, all tables are slightly different because on the whole, organisers use whatever they have to hand.

So although you will normally you may find yourself using the standard 6x2, you might have a different length or width or even a round table (occasionally) because they do tend to use what is available. So be prepared to adapt your display on the day.

I find that it is easier to make up the display with a variety smaller stands that can be adapted to make the best use of the space and shape available, rather than be restricted with a design that will only fit a certain size and shape of stall. Smaller display stands are also easier to pack and carry!

Many fairs also supply electricity, although with some you have to book it specifically. This means that you can light your product, which is well worth doing as it will attract attention. You will need to carry extension cables as well as your lights, some but not all organisers supply the electricity to your stall.

The table is your shop window. And in exactly the same way as a shop window display in the High Street or shopping mall, it has to attract the attention of your potential customer.

It has to help you compete against the stalls on either side of you and opposite you, as well as anyone else selling a similar product.

With any type of selling, whether it's a full page advert in a magazine costing thousands of pounds, or your craft stall - you only have a few seconds to catch the attention of the passing crowd, so you have to make a good first impression that will make your public take that all important second look.

## The Basics

What are the basic elements that you need to turn an often tatty table into an inspiring sales space?

A Cover
Height
Display stands
Lighting

## The Cover

The first layer of your shop window is your cover, the table cloth. Use it to make your stand different.

Make sure that it is big enough to cover your table to the floor at the front and sides – sheeting bought from a fabric shop is ideal as you can buy enough to make a cover for a 6ft or even a 12ft table, and remember, it's better to have your cover too large than too small. If it's too large you can fold and pin it (a good supply of safety pins is invaluable) whereas if it's too small – it won't fit!

A good table cloth keeps your stand neat, creates your image and forms a stock room under the table while the top of the table becomes your selling space, your shop in effect.

A cover that finishes midway down to the floor, showing all the stock boxes that you have stored underneath looks very amateurish and gives the immediate first impression that you don't really know what you're doing. It also looks tatty and remember – first impressions count.

So invest in a good table cover rather than just grabbing the first table cloth or sheet you can find on your way out of the house.

Choose a base colour on which you can build your display. It can make your stand immediately different from your neighbours

The best way to get a cloth that will create the image you want and cover your whole table to the ground at least at the front, is to make your own from sheeting. Ideally you require 3 metres of 300cm extra wide sheeting. Then you simply have to hem the raw edge, drape it over your table and go to work. If sewing a hem is beyond your needlework skills, you can get some hem binding and create a neat edge with an iron.

You can use this simple, standard item to create the image you want for your stand and your business. The basic colour that you choose will form a major part of your overall image.

Pristine white
Warm cream
Eye catching yellow
Attention grabbing red
Elegant blue
Nature loving brown
Sophisticated black

You can also decorate the cloth if you wish to make it more relevant to your craft or product. For instance, if your product includes some form of embroidery, why not embroider a border for the front of your stand.

Stencilling, fabric painting, beadwork, stamping, all these crafts could be used on the actual cloth, while other crafts would lend themselves to forming other types of decoration on the stand. If woodwork is your craft, make sure that the table top stands are of the highest quality. If papercraft, you can make your packaging stand out.

You should also keep your cloth in good condition. Make sure you keep it clean and iron it. Some fabrics crease more easily than others – avoid them if you can, but you want your shop window to look professional and well finished – not all crumpled as if you just dragged it from the wash basket!

## The Height

Once you have the groundwork set, you have to decide on how to display your goods.

Clearly this depends to a very large extent on the product itself. Are you selling small, delicate items or large, flat or three dimensional crafts?

A good basic rule to work by is that people tend to notice things that are at eye level. Brands spend a fortune to obtain the eye level shelving position in supermarkets.

So you want to draw their attention to your display by forming some kind of higher background leading inwards towards the main display.

There are a variety of ways to do this.

You could choose a table top, folding exhibition unit if you want to invest a few hundred pounds in your display. This is in many ways the easiest path to choose and of course it will look very professional, but likewise you would have to be setting up in a very professional manner to warrant this kind of capital outlay in the early stages of your business.

It's easier and far less expensive to make your own stand. And of course it adds to the overall image of a high quality hand crafted product.

There are a number of ways to add dimension to your flat table top.

You can position boxes and drape them with additional, smaller cloths that are the same as or combine well with your main cloth, and create height in that way. Or you can stay with the boxes but decorate them separately and use them on top of the cloth.

You can build a framework to stand at the back of the table. This works basically like a large open book standing at right angles and can be made of two notice boards hinged together, or it can be a more open structure such as trellis held in a frame.

You can design this part of your stand so that your lighting will clip to your frame or to allow for free standing spot lights. Lighting that is directed down onto the display is a very effective style of illuminations and avoids the problem of blinding your customer. Many products can be transformed from something rather ordinary into a glittering Aladdin's Cave with some simple light and again, it will make your stand look professional.

You can also have individual stands for smaller items such as jewellery or ceramic ornaments, or a rail effect if you are selling clothing. Just remember that you must have permission if you want to use a stand additional to your table space and you will normally have to pay for the extra space. Do remember to take you neighbours into account, you should never encroach on their space or block customers from their stand.

You can also buy a selection of clear acrylic stands in various shapes and sizes and these can be very effective for smaller products.

Look around and think out of the box. There are lots of cup cake stands around at the moment and they can make very effective display stands for small items.

Whatever you choose, you should try to avoid the single level, table top display - people don't always look down - they look around as they walk though the hall or marquee and you need to catch their attention as they wander.

But also remember that you have to be able to carry and assemble the display. Always keep that in mind as you create elaborate creations in your imagination!

## Lighting

It's very tempting to ignore lighting, especially when you are first starting out, but that is a mistake.

Think of the way jewellery glitters in jewellery shop windows. It's not just the fact that they are diamonds, gemstones and precious metals, they are also very professionally lit!

And when you look at other stands around you at your first craft show, you will notice that those crafters who know what they are doing - have lights!

When you are deciding on your lights, there are certain things to take into account. They need to be sturdy and easy to carry around. Take the weight into account as well, you will have to carry them from fair to fair and at times, you will have to carry them upstairs to the hotel ballroom or the length of long marquees.

Look around at various shops for your lights. You don't need to go for special - and normally expensive - professional shop display lighting. Nowadays, you can find plenty of choice in home decor or office supply stores.

The style of lighting will depend on your overall display. If you have a large sturdy framework, you can clip lights to that. If your display is more open, you probably need freestanding lights.

The right lighting will really make your stand and your beautiful, handmade designs stand out. And remember, the first part of making a sale is getting a customer's attention in the first place.

You will also need to have extension cables in your equipment pack, as you will often have to connect to the power supply at a distance.

Many organisers will require that you have your electrical equipment tested. A PAT certificate (portable appliance testing) is required for each piece of equipment and lasts 12 months.

There are all sorts of other things, you can add to your stand to attract attention and what you choose will depend on your style.

You could decide to display one of your main pieces on a Lazy Susan so that it catches the light as it turns, or you could use a digital photo frame to showcase some of your other designs..

## Exhibition Banners

However you design your table, the first task of your stand is to be noticed.

You may well be in hall with 50, 70 or over 100 other craft stalls, so you want people to notice your stand. You want them to stop, look at your designs and of course you want them to buy. But if you don't attract them in the first place none of that can happen.

The exhibition banner displayed behind your table is a great way of doing this. It's an advert that people can see from a distance. You can include pictures of your handcrafted pieces on the banner so that they have an idea of what you have on offer before they risk becoming too close!

Many of the copy and print centres and some of the big stationery stores now produce this kind of banner or stand for you from about £60. So if you're planning on doing a number of events this can be a very good investment. Do think of the design carefully. If you use a banner this will be your largest visual advert, so you want to make sure that it is sending the message you want and that it is giving people the correct idea about your style.

## The rest of your equipment bag

There are other things that you need to make sure you have with you when you set out to do a show.

A cash float. Yes, I know the plan is to take money, but you also need to have some with you in the first place. Most people get their money from cash machines nowadays, so they will be presenting you with beautifully crisp £10 and £20 notes, you will need to have some change for them if you want to make a sale. Make sure you have a good selection of £5 notes, £1 coins, silver and copper if you're going to set your prices at £4.99, £9.99, £14.99 etc.

You also want to keep your cash safe. So you will need a cash box to make it easy to sort out your coins, and a bag that you can keep attached to you to keep all the hundreds of £10 notes safe!

As your business grows you might decide to allow customers to pay with their credit or debit card. As technology changes there are a number of different ways of doing this and you will have to research them to find out what will suit you. You will find other crafters that do take plastic and most of them will be very willing to give you the information you need. Each area will vary slightly.

You'll need some extra items in your kit bag. A calculator to add up all the sales, a note book to keep a record of them and also to take details for special orders that you will be sending out, so of course you'll need a pen! If you take a lot of special orders, you could decide to design an order form so you and your customer have a written record of the order.

Depending on how you have decided to display your craft you might need a supply of price labels, some paper bags or gift bags and tissue paper for packaging, or you might need a supply of the gift boxes that you will be using so that you can keep topping up your display as you make sales.

Then there are some useful small extras – scissors, safety pins, sticky tape and of course, plenty of business cards or leaflets.

If you're working on your own, you'll need to take some food and drink with you as you might not be able to leave your stall. Once you get used to the fairs you are doing you will know if food is available easily or if you can ask your neighbour to watch things for you. Some organisers don't allow you to eat at your stand – and I wouldn't recommend sitting down to a large meal at any event, but a sandwich and a bottle of water can keep you going through a long day. Although the show might be open to the public from 10–4, you will probably be there from 8 -5 – and then there's your travelling time. They can be very long days!

## To show or not to show?

Now that you have your stand structure organised you have to decide how to place your product on it.

There is a great temptation to put absolutely everything on display at the same time, but you should avoid this.

Use the curtained space you have created beneath the table as your stock room and the table top for the presentation of your product.

The way you present your display has a direct effect on the way it is seen by the customer. Not just in a straight forward visual way but subconsciously as well.

In general, a crowded display tends to imply that the product is cheap. Think of the `pile them high, sell them cheap' methods of some supermarkets. They don't just choose that style by accident, a lot of money has gone into researching the effect it has on the image of the product or the retailer.

At the other end of the scale, think of the way high quality, expensive products are displayed in the department stores. A single piece of crystal will stand on its own, the window display will present two or three outfits in a set piece. The space left around the product is as important as the product itself if you want to create an image of quality.

So the general rule is:-

A cluttered effect - bargain basement prices and low quality products

A very elegant display - high quality and high prices

You probably want to pitch your product somewhere between the two. After all, you want to get the right price but you don't want to scare people off!

Another very good reason for keeping some of the stock back in reserve is to encourage a customer to *buy now*.

If the potential customer sees only one example of the glass, jumper, picture or teddy bear that they particularly like, they are more likely to purchase it straight away rather than leave it until later, because it might be gone when they get back.

This is doubly important. It means that you get the sale straight away, and it avoids the problem of the well meaning customer never returning to make the purchase.

# Making a Sale

You have chosen your craft, designed and made your product, set your prices, booked your craft fair and set up your stall. Now what?

You have to make your sales.

It's not enough simply to be there and hope that your product sells itself - very few items do and if you don't prepare yourself for the actual process of selling you will be letting your whole venture down. Selling is nowhere near as terrifying as some people fear and at a craft fair you will simply be talking to people who have already shown an interest in your product.

In fact, it can be a great confidence booster when complete strangers praise your work!

Prepare beforehand to give the best service you can to your customer.

Make sure that you have enough change easily available - there's nothing worse than scrabbling around in your pockets or bag looking for coins, even worse if you have to ask a neighbouring stallholder.

Make sure that you look smart - but at the same time take some trouble to make sure that you will be comfortable. Standing all day behind your stand can be awful in uncomfortable shoes, and marquees can be very draughty and bitterly cold or extremely hot. I find it's best to use layering, wear a jacket, cardigan or jumper that you can take off. In the winter, probably all three plus a hat!

If you're going to be on your own, take a drink and something to eat so that you do not have to leave the stand, but try not to make it look like you have set up a picnic!

Price everything clearly. People like to know how much something is before they get sucked into asking questions and being pressurised. Not marking your prices can simply scare customers off, making them assume that if it isn't priced it must be expensive.

Have your bags or boxes easily accessible - you don't want to go disappearing under the stand for five minutes while you search around for your packaging.

Have something printed about yourself that makes you look more businesslike, after all this is not a car boot sale, you should want your customers to be able to find you so that they can make further purchases.

If you have a number of fairs booked, print a leaflet with a list of the dates and events where you can be found. Customers like to be able to follow you from fair to fair and having a list that they can keep makes it easy for them to find you at the next event. Many of my regular customers visit fairs because I have put them on my diary leaflet, and many of them do not buy on-line even though they have the details – a great number of people still like to be able to feel and see the gifts they are buying.

If it is appropriate to your product, think about having a simple brochure or leaflet produced so that they can make further orders. Or have business cards available giving your telephone number or address to help your customer to buy from you again – some DO buy on-line!

When a potential customer does approach your stand, you have to look approachable.

*Do not* hide yourself behind your display as if you don't want to be disturbed.

*Do not* slump and look fed up - even if you are.

*Do not* be engrossed in a conversation with your friend or neighbouring stallholder.

Try to look interested in them - without looking too desperate to shake their money out of them.

Smile to let them know that you have seen them, let them look without leaping up to hover over them – that's why it's better to stand than sit behind your stall – leaning forward slightly is much less intimidating than actually standing up.

If someone is taking more than a passing interest, that is the time to involve yourself in conversation. Point out something about your product. If it reflects the light- lift it up to show them, if it has some movement - demonstrate it.

Find something that works for your product, something that gives you an excuse to pick it up and involve the customer. Once you have formed this initial connection it becomes much easier to convert interest into a sale.

Be open when they ask you questions, be interested in them, make parting with their money a pleasure - if it's not, why should they part with it?

Think about how you would like to be treated if you were considering buying yourself a treat

## Setting your stall

There is no one best way of setting out your stand. No matter how many fairs and events you have done, each one is slightly different, and although you'll develop a general layout for your stand, don't let it get too set in concrete.

Different rooms will create a different flow of people – sometimes they will approach you from the left, sometimes from the right. I like to set my show stopper pieces at the far end of my stand as they approach. I find that this will stop them and then they look back along the rest of the stand, but if I put it at the beginning, they have walked past before they notice. People are normally looking at eye level and slightly ahead.

I also place the small impulse buy items flat on the table and starting close to the first point they reach, because I find that once a browser notices the stand they will then look down – it means they don't have to make eye contact if they find they're not interested in your items!

So I adapt my display to the space that I find myself in at different fairs, and if things aren't working as well as I'd like, I'll reorganise the display.

Selling is a very important part of the business process. You cannot assume that your work is so good it will just sell itself. Some of it will, but you are in competition for the pound or dollar in the customers pocket and you must work for it.

Don't pounce on anyone who pauses at your stand, you will frighten them off. But don't simply ignore them either. Smile. Say hello, show them that you are actually interested rather than just bored!

You should understand your product – after all you designed and made it! So be prepared to explain it if a potential customer asks questions. Even if you feel that they are simply wasting your time, the fact that you are answering questions, explaining your design, showing how it works, will attract other people who also wanted to know but didn't like to ask – and they might buy from you.

## Finishing off the sale in style

Once you have interested them enough to make a sale, package your product attractively. Invest in smart bags and tissue paper rather than newspaper or old supermarket carriers!

The packaging you use depends on your product. You might be able to use boxes and ribbon to make your hand painted china look even more special, or you could use small gift bags for smaller items. Do remember that packaging matters - that's why we buy designer perfume! Even simple packaging has a purpose – it reflects the image you are trying to create.

The very process of packaging can make the item seem even more special and precious.

Have your tissue paper, ribbons and gift bags within easy reach – you can set up a small table behind your stall for packaging. Think about how they wrap things in the department store for Christmas. 'Would you like it

Gift Wrapped?' and then they proceed to make an event out of the wrapping, making a bottle of perfume seem much more special. Certainly more special than simply stuffing it into a carrier bag! And it attracts further sales from those looking on.

Finally, make sure that people can find you again to make more purchases. Put your name or trading title on the product. Have a gift card to slip into the packaging, have a gift tag that you can attach to all your items. Find some way that you can add your name and contact details to every single thing that you sell.

Have cards printed with your details or produce a list of craft fairs that you can be found at in the future and place them on the counter where people can pick them up as they pass.

## The power of the impulse purchase

– many pennies make the pounds.

When you are designing your product range it can be very tempting to concentrate on more expensive items, the pieces that really show your skill and ignore the smaller, cheaper ones, but this is a mistake.

Of course it's always very nice to sell something expensive – and you should certainly try to have some special and expensive pieces in your range, they are the designs that will attract the attention in the first place, but many of your sales will be at the smaller end of the scale.

In recessions, the big fashion houses find that lipsticks and nail varnishes sell really well.

Why?

Why would you spend £25 on a lipstick if money is tight?

It's because you might not be able to afford a new designer outfit or bag – but you can still give yourself a treat with a designer lipstick!

So don't ignore the power of the impulse buy.

It's tempting to think that the real profit is in the expensive item on your stall but often the opposite is true. The star of the show might well be the crowd puller - and on that basis alone it will have earned its keep - but at the end of the day when you check your records you will probably find that it is the small, low priced, easily packaged item that has made the real money.

Pocket money purchases, a little gift for the tourists to take home, a small extra gift for Christmas, something to take home for Mum. This is the type of sale that really adds up and you will almost certainly find that this is where the real profit lies.

If your range is based on higher value products it is probably going to be worth your while to give some thought to how you can adapt your craft to the small impulse purchase. After all, the designer accessories are much better sellers than the couture suits, even for the likes of Chanel and Christian Dior. As always - learn from the experts.

Of course, if you are going to charge less you must remember to make sure that it also cost you less to make.

Work out how you can increase the speed you can make them at. Will you save time by doing each stage on a number of items at a time rather than working on each one individually from start to finish, think of it as a mini production line.

Not everyone goes to a fair intending or able to buy a wrought iron table, but many more could be tempted by a candle holder.

## Making Valuable Contacts

While you are at a craft event it is important to realise that there may be other sales opportunities available to you as well as an immediate sale on the day. With some crafts it is as important to make contacts as it is to find an immediate sale.

Every time you set up your stand at a craft fair you are putting your product in front of the general public and you should take every advantage of that.

Of course, the main object of being at a craft fair is to sell your product to those people on that day and to go home with some money, but it's not the only object. You should also be prepared to receive requests for special orders, from someone with a shop who wants to stock your product and even a contract for a larger event.

Think about your product in a wider context and try to see if it has potential for gaining you a larger order.

If you create displays of dried flowers you could supply a number of your arrangements for an office building, hotel or restaurant, or someone may ask you for a number of arrangements in a special colour for a party or wedding.

If your craft is soft furnishing, you may find a potential client who requires much more than the odd cushion - a new house to design, a special event to decorate, an upmarket bed & breakfast to dress. Designer ceramics could be just the touch a restaurant was looking for to make a special impression. Safe and interesting toys could be exactly the thing for a kindergarten, or your pictures precisely the image a new beauty salon has been searching for.

If you think that your product does have wider potential, it is probably worth spending some time on doing some initial research and possible even promoting the idea to potential customers.

You must be prepared for the opportunity when it comes along, and you already have the information you need to work out your wholesale prices.

When you worked out your costs originally, you learnt how much each item actually costs in parts and how much time it takes to make, this means that you can work out what your minimum price should be, still allowing for some profit. The idea of offering a reduction for a larger order is that you can afford to give a discount because you are able to sell a larger amount at one time and reduce your selling cost. But you still want some profit.

This is the basic information you need to be able to produce a price list for larger orders – basically, your wholesale pricelist.

It enables you to calculate how much discount you can afford to give, or how much commission you can pay someone else to sell for you.

You also have to take into account some of the extra costs that can be involved in taking a larger order. You might need some extra help to make the items, you might have to actually purchase more parts than you had planned for or you might have to invest in another piece of equipment.

A larger order might be the stepping stone you've been looking for to grow your business to the next stage or it might simply be too large for you at this particular stage of your business. No matter how good an order looks, it's only worth having if you make a profit.

You must also decide if you will invoice for an order and give credit.

This will cost you money in paperwork, waiting time and unfortunately there is always the possibility of late payment and even bad debt. This must be calculated into your prices. As a basic rule, avoid offering credit until you have built up a working relationship with someone.

In other opportunities, especially when you are putting your craft into another outlet to sell to the public, such as a craft shop, the business model might involve selling on commission, paying rent for the space used to display your items, or sale or return.

In any of these models you are still taking the risk rather than the seller. They are not placing an order for your craft they are giving you the opportunity to sell through their outlet. If it sells you pay a commission or they pay you the agreed wholesale price – if it doesn't sell you get your stock back.

If you do choose to work with this model you have to be sure that the terms are clearly understood by both sides and that you are able to trust the people you will be working with. After all you could be handing over stock worth a lot of money! So although it can seem very tempting to jump at the chance or extra sales, do your homework before making your decision.

## Personalised orders.

There is a big difference between a wholesale order or large contract and a bespoke order.

A bespoke order – for instance for a wedding or large party – is still a large order but the customer isn't necessarily looking for a discount. Indeed, if you are personalising your design or creating it in a special colour, you may actually be able to charge more than your normal price. Having something made to your specific requirements carries a premium in any business.

As a crafter you are perfectly placed to be able to create personalised items and it can be very lucrative.

There are many people who love to be able to have something made or designed personally for them – whether it is a piece of jewellery, a piece of furniture or the soft furnishings for their designer house.

There are different things to take into account when thinking about taking orders for bespoke or personalised work and you should think about them before you are faced with a potential customer.

Some crafts are obvious candidates for personalised work. Cakemaking, jewellery, soft furnishings or handcrafted cards can all be promoted as bespoke orders and you should think about whether you want to promote your craft in this area. If you do, you should make some decisions about how you will handle an enquiry and order before you actually reach the craft fair.

There are a number of things to take into account.

When will you require payment – full payment on placing the order or just a deposit?

If a customer places a special order that you would have difficulty selling elsewhere – special colours or even personalised with someone's name – take full payment or at least a deposit that is large enough to cover your costs, at the time the order is placed.

You also have to take into account that a special order for a particular colour will probably mean that you have to buy special parts and you will possibly have to place a minimum order with your supplier.

You'll have to decide if it's worth placing an order for a hundred of a special colour when you only need 20 for the order you are quoting for. Will you be able to sell the rest when you make them up or is the potential customer asking for a very unusual colour that you don't think you'll find another market for? If that's the case, the customer's special order will have to pay for the entire consignment because you could find yourself stuck with the rest of them.

Are you going to produce a sample first or just deliver the finished order?

Finally, if you have to send an order out to the customer, remember that it will cost extra to pack it and post it. You must include this in your calculation..

If you get all this right and make sure that you look businesslike and your product looks professional in the first place, you could end up with the most profitable craft fair of your life.

Many crafts lend themselves more easily than others to personalisation and special orders. Celebration cakes are an obvious area where a large part of your business could come from special orders.

Many people also like to have bespoke jewellery pieces made for them and of course wedding jewellery can be a large part of a handmade jewellery business.

If you make handcrafted cards, produce a leaflet that promotes your party and wedding invitation service.

If your craft is home decor could you promote your service for designing bijou bed & breakfast furnishings or creating designer nurseries for new babies?

You might think it's obvious, but most people need to have the idea put in front of them – that's why companies spend millions on advertising.

So if this is an area you would like to explore design a small leaflet or brochure for your business, showing how you can personalise your designs for a special order or event. It could lead your craft business in an entirely new direction.

# Other selling opportunities

So far I have concentrated on selling at craft fairs, but as I mentioned at the beginning there are many other opportunities for selling face-to-face and once you have learnt how to present yourself and set up your storefront you can use the same skills at many other events.

School and church fairs
Charity events
Country shows
Christmas markets
Wedding fairs
House parties
Markets
Talks to groups
Demonstrations at shows

### School and church fairs.

These are obviously held at local schools and churches. They are quite often much shorter events than a standard craft fair, possibly only two or three hours during the afternoon or in the evening. They can also be midweek whereas most craft fairs are held at the weekends. This means that they are easy to fit in around your main schedule and are good way to expand your selling hours.

Although they are much smaller events, attracting a much smaller number of people, they are often very well attended by people who have every intention of purchasing from you. Most of them will also cost you a lot less in stall rent, although you often have to supply a raffle prize – think of it as an advert.

They tend to be held at certain times of the year such as Easter, in the summer and in the lead up to Christmas.

Many of the organisers visit established craft fairs to find potential exhibitors for these smaller events, which is another reason that you should have business cards and information to give out at fairs.

Once you are on an organisers list they will be happy for you to become a regular exhibitor, doing the same fairs year after year, hopefully attracting a loyal following. Many charity events also fall into this pattern although some of them are larger and are held in hotels rather than the school or Church hall.

## Country shows

Country shows, town fairs or big events such as air shows and flower festivals often have a craft marquee as part of the overall event.

The way this is organised can vary enormously and depends on the type of show that you are looking at.

For instance a local country show can be organised by a committee of local people, while some of the large flower festivals are organised by the Royal Horticultural

Society and the craft marquee at these large events are very often organised separately within the overall event by one of the major national craft guilds or associations.

If a show is being organised by local committee, you simply apply as you would with any other event. But if it's being organised by a craft guild you will almost certainly need to be a member of that particular guild. You will have to make enquiries of each event you are interested in.

Many of these events – whoever organises them, - are held in marquees, hopefully, but not necessarily in good weather, so you should be prepared for whatever the weather throws at you!

In fact being prepared is a vital part of being able to make a success of this type of show. Check the weather forecast and dress for the event. Spending an extended amount of time in a marquee can be either very cold or very hot, unfortunately it's rarely comfortably in the middle.

So have either warm clothes and waterproof shoes or a fan! Layering is a very good idea when you're working in a marquee, because it may start out cold but then get hot or vice versa. You also have to take into account that marquee shows can be cancelled if the weather is really bad. Some of our recent wet summers have caused havoc with the events calendar and this can have a disastrous effect on your cash flow if you have been depending on the income from a small number of large events.

Most of the big country shows will last at least two days although many of them can be spread over three or four days and some last up to a full week, so you need to make sure that you have plenty of stock with you. Plan for each day being excellent, if you have one or two slow days you will have some stock left but that is much better than running out of products to sell.

The rent for this type of show can also vary enormously depending on whether it is a local event or a large national event.

Some organisers will require you to sign quite detailed contracts and it is worth reading these to make sure that you know exactly what you are committing yourself to. Of course you would never sign anything without reading it fully - would you!

One part to check very carefully is the clause on cancellation.

There are some organisers will not refund your rent even if they cancel the event and this could result in you losing a large upfront investment, possibly the cost of accommodation and of course the loss of the opportunity to sell altogether for that weekend. Personally I refuse to book any event with this cancellation clause in the contract - I disagree with it on principle!

These larger events are a significant investment in time and money, and only you will be able to decide whether it suits you or not and what stage in your business it might suit you.

When they work, large shows can bring in large amounts of money and be very worthwhile, but it's probably not a good idea to rely on them totally, certainly not in the early stage of your business.

You can never guarantee an income in any business, but literally putting all your eggs in one basket can be very financially dangerous.

## Christmas markets.

Christmas markets are quite obviously held at Christmas.

They have become very popular in recent years and they tend to be organised by towns and cities and are held as part of the general Christmas festivities.

Although they do vary from town to town, many of them last a number of weeks and take the form of market stalls in the town or city centre. Sometimes they are standard market stalls under canvas, but some towns set up individual wooden huts to become individual mini shops and others set aside a section of an indoor market or shopping mall.

If the stalls are outside you have to be prepared for the weather if you do this type of event.

Being outside in winter can certainly be cold but it can also be wet so you need to make sure that your work is protected if the rain or snow would damage it.

You will probably also have to setup and dismantle your stall each day, as obviously you cannot leave anything open overnight in the middle of a town centre.

If you are concentrating on Christmas, make sure that you present your product as a potential Christmas present.

Learn from the big stores in the way that they present their Christmas stock - they create a range of products which can be simply picked up and presented as a complete present, often without even having to gift wrap it.

Although you don't have to create designs that are only suitable for Christmas - whether that is a range of Christmas tree earrings, cheery robins painted on your ceramics or snow covered scenery on your soft furnishings - you should definitely present your craft as a Christmas present. You could offer free gift wrapping, package them as collections in beautiful boxes or in organza bags with Christmas tags attached.

Another thing to remember is that people do have birthdays and anniversaries and other events during the Christmas season, and it can sometimes be very difficult to find anything in the stores that is not packaged as a Christmas present. So it is well worth while creating gift packaging that is not overtly Christmas.

## Wedding fairs.

Wedding fairs are very specific events.

But that doesn't mean that you cannot adapt your craft to suit this market.

If you are a jeweller or a papercrafter, if you make cupcakes, occasion cakes, work with silk flowers or create soft furnishings, your craft can easily be adapted to suit the huge and hugely profitable wedding market.

If you haven't been involved in the wedding process yourself recently, invest in some of the wedding magazines to see the huge range of products that are now involved in a modern wedding. You can adapt almost any craft to the wedding industry.

Special orders and bespoke designs are vital part of working in this area.

In the bridal shop the bride has to choose from the designs that are available, and although there can be hundreds of designs, they are all quite similar. But when she comes to you she can have a design created specifically for her, including the colours and style she wants for her wedding.

This can be a very interesting and lucrative area to specialise in.

Wedding fairs are very often held at wedding venues such as hotels, Country Houses and Civic Centres. You will find that there is quite a difference in the cost of a wedding fair as opposed to a craft fair. A six-foot table at a craft fair could cost £50, while the same six-foot table in the same room at a wedding fair could cost you £150.

You will also need to think specifically about how you design your table for a wedding fair.

The event itself is different, other stallholders will not be other crafters, they will be professional photographers, wedding dress shops, printers who specialise in wedding stationery, suppliers of wedding cars, event organisers, make-up artists and hairdressers.

Many of them will have the professional display stands and the equipment that they use in their shops. This doesn't mean that you have to suddenly invest thousands of pounds in professional shopfitting equipment, but it does mean that you will have to present yourself very professionally.

If you use white cloths make sure that they are a good heavy quality and are spotlessly clean. Although many people choose white, you might decide to stand out from the crowd by using a colour. It's entirely your choice, but many things show up beautifully against a rich royal blue or deep burgundy.

Although it's wonderful to make sales actually at the event, a wedding fair is mainly about future sales and getting orders, so it is absolutely vital that you have plenty of information for the bride to take away with her.

As already mentioned, most of your fellow exhibitors will be wedding professionals, but your shouldn't see this as a negative, it can be a great opportunity for you stand out from the crowd – in a good way of course!

Many of the other stands will be manned (or womaned!) by people who work for the company rather than those who actually own it. And a lot of them will simply sit behind their stands expecting potential clients to pick up their leaflets. At the other extreme, others will be at the side of their stand shoving their leaflets into any hand that passes, whether the person shows any interest or not.

You will have a chance to be different.

Smile at people, engage with them, talk to them. Exhibiting at the wedding fair is all about making connections with people so that they will remember you and so that you will have the opportunity to contact them.

Gathering a list of contacts is vital, because very often, a bride and groom will be looking for ideas for the wedding that can be up to 2 years in the future. So you need to be able to keep in contact with them. Collect names and addresses and e-mail addresses, and the date of their wedding so that you can target your marketing to suit their timescale. But also be aware that many brides arrange everything well in advance – buying a dress two years ahead and then having to worry about staying the right size!

Make arrangements for a home visit if it's relevant to discuss exactly what is wanted – and to get a signature on an order form.

Don't be afraid to talk about how far ahead you get fully booked! Sometimes you have to persuade a bride that she needs to make sure she won't miss out on your perfect part of her wedding. And don't ignore the Bride's mother – she has a lot to do with the decisions, and she might well be paying your account!

You will have put a lot of effort and expense into being at the wedding fair – don't let potential clients slip away. They might seems absolutely convinced when you talk to them, but you need to get them to commit to you – if you don't, someone at next week's wedding fair will!

So be prepared to take orders or make reservations on the day. Create a booking or order form and have them ready to use.

Don't be afraid of having slightly quirky designs. After all, a bride who simply wants white pearls and silver crystals can buy her jewellery from hundreds of different places, so can the bride who wants a typical 3 tier wedding cake, or the same style of flowers that all her friends have chosen.

The bride who wants something different is much more likely to notice you if you don't just display the traditional designs and ideas.

As with all parts of your hand crafted business, you can't possibly be all things to all people. Even if you could produce every style of jewellery or every colour and style of bouquet, favour, wedding photography, stationary or table decoration - you can't produce enough of it to sell to everybody.

So you may as well specialise in a niche that you enjoy and become a big player in a small niche. Some of my most successful wedding jewellery designs have featured rich colours such as Amethyst, deep red Garnets or rich and vibrant orange carnelian. While not every bride wants to stick to the traditional pale whites and ivories, it's not always easy to find a bridal tiara that features rich purple Amethyst.

When doing wedding stationary, one of my favourite orders featured dragons – trying getting that in your local stationary shop!

One of your main selling points is that you are the creator of unique handmade designs rather than a seller of mass produced standard pieces. So have a selection of your designs and colours. This means that you will be able to show the bride the various colours or styles that she could choose from.

You can also personalise your items, if you're a jeweller, you could even make a small hair clip for her using these colours and attach it to your business card as a gift.

Actually making or decorating items at your stand will always attract attention – although not if your craft makes too much noise or is too messy – you don't want a constantly running sewing machine making noise all day or pots of paint next to wedding dresses – you won't be popular!

Think about how you could adapt your craft and how you could display it to attract a bride and her order.

## Home and furnishing shows

Many crafts lend themselves to shows aimed at improving the look and style of your home.

Soft furnishings, wall art, photography, handmade furniture, wrought iron work, garden ornaments, ceramics and glass and many other crafts as well as homemade produce are ideally suited to this type of show.

Many of these events are large annual events held in the major exhibition centres around the country. Others are held as part of other large events such as flower shows and large country shows.

If you do choose this type of event you will be competing with large manufacturers and companies, not other crafters, so your costs will be much higher, but they can still be worthwhile, especially if you specialise in very high end unique designs. You don't need many sales of £1,000+ to make it worth exhibiting!

Although you will still be handcrafting your items, you will have to be very professional before approaching most large shows and events in this area as you will be competing as a business not a crafter. But it can be an ideal way to take your business to the next level. You are not only putting your products in front of the public, you are placing them in front of other businesses who might like to stock your designs.

## House parties

Selling by party plan at house parties can be a very successful way of selling your handmade creations.

Some of the more traditional party plan has gone out of fashion, after all there is only so much food storage that you really want! But that doesn't mean that the idea of party plan is out of date, far from it, it just means that people are looking for more unusual reasons to have a party.

Many unique handmade items are ideal for this.

Most of them are a very easy present to give to others and you can have enough of a price range to make it comfortable for everybody at the party. Because although some people can quite comfortably afford to spend £70 or £80, in these more economically challenging times there are many others who would be relieved to be able to just spend £5 or £10 without embarrassment – so make sure that you have a wide spread of values.

Once you have started doing house parties, they do have a tendency to feed off themselves, in fact that's the whole idea of a successful party plan business. Someone, preferably two people at the party will book parties of their own and invite different selections of people, which will lead on again to more bookings and more new customers.

Obviously the best way to start is if you can persuade some of your friends to hold a party for you. But you can also arrange to work with someone who already does party plan with a different product and is willing to let you join them.

You should also advertise the fact that you do parties at every other event that you attend. I have arranged many parties with customers at a craft fair, talking to them about it as I am packaging their purchase. After all, if they've have bought something from you they already know and like your work

There are a few main things you need to do, to create a successful party plan business.

### Make it easy for the host to have a party.

Create invitations or leaflets that they can hand out to their friends.

People need to know what to expect to see for sale at the party and how much they expect the items to cost, so that they have an idea of the price ranges. They also need to know when and where it is. It's a good idea to put some photos of your work onto the invitation and if you have a website put the address on so that they can go and have a look at the type of hand crafted items you have for sale. And do emphasise that it is handmade, by you rather than just mass produced and available at the local market.

### Make it worthwhile for the host to have a party.

She will be going to quite a lot of trouble and some expense, providing wine and nibbles, or tea and cake at least for her guests, as well as putting the time in to arrange the party. So it has to be worth her while. You can decide on the exact style of your incentive, but generally it will be something like a percentage of the value of your total sales in the evening to be spent on her own order. The percentage is up to you, but is normally somewhere between 10% and 20%. You could also decide to give a bonus for each person that books a further party, or a special offer only available to the organiser on the evening. The more creative you can be, the more successful you should be in booking future parties. After all, people are more likely to book a party of their own if they feel it's going to be worthwhile to them.

### Make it easy to set up your party.

For both your sake and your host's sake, you don't want to spend two hours setting up your display! Design an easy and time efficient way of carrying and setting out your range. You have a limited amount of time and space when doing a house party, so don't try to take every design you've ever made. Decide from your experience, what your bestsellers are and make sure that you have them, together with enough variety for people to have a choice, but not so much that it overwhelms them.

### Make it interesting for the host and her guests.

Don't just put your items out and expect it to sell itself. Don't just stand in a corner like a wallflower. Give a short talk that explains something about your craft, what makes it special, what makes it different?

Give them an idea of the price range, talk about how you can design special pieces for them. How bracelets can be made at a size to suit, how you can design soft furnishing to match their existing decor, how you can personalise a hand painted teaset, create unique stationary for a party or recreate a much loved teddy.

A party is entertainment and you need the focus to be on you and your products rather than just leaving them to chat amongst themselves and forget about you.

### Make it easy for the guests to make a purchase.

Most party plan businesses rely on people placing an order and receiving it at a later date. Personally I always have my selection of handmade jewellery for them to take away on the night, and you can do this with a number of different crafts. I don't like to rely on delayed gratification – most people like to be able to take their purchase home with them. Of course there are some crafts that don't fit this pattern, or where a significant proportion of your work is personalised and will have to be created especially for the client.

If someone does want a special order, I will normally take the order and send or deliver the piece directly to them rather than expecting the host of the party to do the deliveries for me.

### Make it easy to make a booking

Finally make it easy and worthwhile for the guests to book a party of their own. The life blood of a party plan business is to continually book new parties. If you book one party from each party that you do, your business will stay level. If you book two parties from each party you do your business will grow. But if you don't book any parties, your business will die.

## Markets

Many towns hold regular markets. Some of these are general markets, some of them are farmers markets, and some of them are craft markets. Which type you might decide to take a stall at is entirely up to you. Different markets suit different crafters, but there are some general rules that apply to any of them.

Most market organisers will supply the stalls, which are normally a metal framework covered by a (mostly) waterproof canvas. They will also normally supply the table top for you to set your product out on. You will have to supply your own covers, and of course you won't have electricity in most cases.

You will also be outside in all weathers, so if your craft can be damaged by the damp, make sure that you protect it.

Markets take place on every day of the week. Some towns have a weekly market, whereas others are held every day of the week. Many market traders have a weekly route around their local towns, setting up shop every morning in the next town. As a crafter it is highly unlikely that you will follow that pattern as you need time to create your product, so you would probably only do two or maybe three regular days a week.

Some of the indoor markets have space allocated for a specialist Craft fair that they hold once a month. Although these are held in markets, they do follow more the pattern of the craft fair. You will have a 6 foot table as your stall and you probably will have an electrical supply.

Markets - whether indoor or outside - are very open areas, with the public milling around, rather than people who have chosen to come into a craft fair. This means that you can have a much wider range of potential customers, but it also means that you have to be more aware of the risk of shoplifters. Make sure that any expensive pieces are out of the way of sticky fingers and take care of your cash.

If you are planning on doing many markets, it is worth joining the National Market Traders Federation, (in the UK) membership of which gives you public and product liability insurance, as well as many other benefits.

## Talks to social and church groups

There are many groups who are constantly looking for people to give talks at their monthly meetings. These can be in the evenings or during the day and are normally during the week.

Obviously, many of the people who will give talks will require some payment to cover their costs.

If you are able to take a selection of your products with you, and that are available for their members to purchase, then you can offer to give the talk without charge. You are taking the risk that you will give the talk and not take any money, but personally I have never had this happen. In fact, many of these events can be extremely lucrative.

I always give a gift to the organisation that they can use as a raffle prize - sometimes on the night, sometimes with a raffle to be held at a later date - it's their choice. As a crafter, you can give a gift that is worth a lot more than it costs you to produce.

Many members of such groups are members of more than one, so as always, do make sure that everyone has your contact details. As with party plan, you will find that you make bookings from bookings.

Again, as with party plan, make it easy to set up your display.

For both your sake and the group's sake, you don't want to spend two hours setting up your stand! They will often only have access to the hall about half an hour before the start of their meeting. Normally, they will deal with group business, such as reading the minutes, first and then hand the rest of the meeting over to you. You will have to be able to set up your display quickly and quietly. You will also need to be able to pack it away quickly once the meeting is over.

Design an easy and time efficient way of carrying and setting out your range, don't try to take every design you've ever made. You will also have to be flexible about how you set out your display as you might not know beforehand what type of tables they will supply.

Decide from your experience what your bestsellers are and make sure that you have them, together with enough variety for people to have a choice, but not so much that it overwhelms them. You'll find over time that your bestsellers vary from venue to venue and event type to event type. Keep a record of what you sell so that you can see any patterns that emerge.

Make it interesting for the group, you are there to give a talk after all, you are the entertainment. Don't just put your designs out and expect them to sell themselves, selling anything is supposed to be a bonus at this type of event.

Give a short talk that explains something about your craft. What is the history of the craft? What makes your designs special? What makes them different to something mass produced? What attracted you to it, why did you choose craftwork in the first place, how did you learn your skills?

For this type of talk, you can get more personal, because they are not just interested in buying the product they are interested in what drew you into this lifestyle.

How did you learn? How long have you been making and designing? Where do you get your design inspiration? What made you decide to set up business?

Give them an idea of your price range. Show how you can put a set together. Talk about how you can design special pieces for them.

Once you have finished your talk, which you should keep to about 20 to 30 minutes, be prepared for a rush!

This is not a leisurely day long craft fair, everybody wants to be served within about 15 minutes before they rush off to get a bus, meet someone who's giving them a lift, or just get home! If you can, take someone with you to help as you can be bombarded with questions after the talk, so it helps if you have someone who can actually make the sales.

These talks can take place during the day or in the evenings and at any time of the week, depending on what type of group you are talking to. So you can fit quite a number into your calendar. They are often booked over a year in advance as the social secretary arranges the plan for the year so be prepared to plan ahead.

## Demonstrations

Demonstrations are a great way of selling and they can take a number of forms.

Demonstrating shows people that you do actually know what you're doing. They love seeing how something is made, that it is actually a handcrafted piece of jewellery created in front of them, or that you hand colour your cards with watercolours, on sew each bead onto the cushion by hand.

Obviously you have to choose specific parts of your work to demonstrate, you can put small mosaics together but you couldn't build a whole mosaic garden table! But if you can set aside some space to demonstrate you will normally be able to gather a crowd to your stall. Some organisers will give you extra space if you are willing to demonstrate, because they know that this is a draw for the public.

There are also times when you will be asked to simply go and demonstrate your craft. This can be in a craft store, where they want to sell craft equipment. It can be at a school or youth club, where they would like you to teach others how to make items.

One of the benefits of this is that it creates an image for you as an expert in your field, and as well as leading to work demonstrating or teaching, it can also lead to sales and special orders for your handcrafted work.

## Be prepared to expand

So as you can see, there are many different ways of reaching out to your customer in face-to-face situations.

Most people do start out with local craft fairs, but as you begin to do these craft shows, you will find that other opportunities open up to you and you should always make sure that you are prepared for the opportunity.

Many organisers arranging new events or looking for new stallholders for their well-established events, will visit other craft fairs looking for fresh ideas and new designers.

Other organisers will be looking for speakers for their regular meetings or craftspeople who are willing to come to their workplaces, callcentres or nursing homes and set up stall for a few hours. In these cases you will be providing a type of entertainment but they can be very profitable, after all you have a captive audience rather than competing with many other craft stalls on the day. Many of these organisers will visit craft fairs to look for suitable ideas and crafters that they feel able to approach.

Some of these organisers will actually stop to talk to you, but others prefer to simply pick up your business card or leaflet and call you at a later date. So obviously it is very important to have plenty of business cards or leaflets easily available on your stall. They will also be looking for people that are willing to interact with others, so that's another reason why you shouldn't just sit behind your small reading a book and drinking coffee.

If you do have a stand at a number of events, prepare a leaflet that lists them all so that people can follow you around. Regular customers are very valuable and they will also recommend you to their friends.

Include your contact details on this leaflet, your business name, your phone number, your e-mail address and website - but be very careful about putting your geographical address. If you work from home, you are effectively giving people a list of dates when your home will be empty!

If you would like to do party plan or talks, add this to your leaflet. You can also produce a more detailed leaflet about your party plan arrangements, which you can hand out to people if they ask about it.

Also be prepared to discuss wholesale prices if you have decided that you are interested in offering this. You might decide that you don't want to expand too much, that you want to keep tight control over the amount of items that you have time to make. That is entirely up to you. You have started this business to fit your lifestyle, so don't get pushed into an area that you are not really comfortable with.

But selling your designs through other outlets can either help you expand your business or allow you to concentrate on creating rather than doing hundreds of events yourself.

People who run craft and gift shops or who have a selection of handcrafted items for sale in their coffee shops, garden centres, wedding boutiques or spas and hotels need to be able to source these items.

So have the information available if you are interested. It doesn't have to be a printed wholesale price list or an official catalogue - you're not a major wholesaler after all - you create handcrafted items. But it can be a lucrative area to explore and you should consider what your response will be to such an enquiry.

Can you produce enough items to sell through someone else? How many are you able or prepared to produce? What are your wholesale prices? Would you be interested in placing your designs somewhere and selling on commission? These are all business decisions and depend entirely on your own business plan and circumstances.

Many people see selling at craft fairs as the launch pad for a much larger, more production led business. Others see it as a business format that they can control and enjoy, keeping the size and the time invested limited so that it fits in with other areas of their individual life style.

There is no right or wrong way to plan the future of your craft business, after all you have set it up to suit you and your lifestyle, and that's exactly what it should do.

# How much stock to make

Once you have done a number of craft fairs – and kept your records – you will begin to see how much you are selling of each item or type of product in your range.

When you have those figures you will be able to calculate how much stock to make.

You must have enough stock to sell.

It sounds obvious but it's terrible to run out in the middle of a fair, knowing that you could have sold more if only you had it!

Of course, everyone would love to be able to go home with empty stock boxes and it's very rare that it actually happens – infact if it does you've probably made a mistake in your stock levels, unless you make edibles – they often sell out, but for the rest of us it isn't normally a problem.

But what is a problem, is that it's far too easy to run out of the most popular item in your range, and not only does that lose you potential sales of that particular design, it might mean that you lose other sales if your best seller is also the one that attracts attention in the first place. That's why it is so important to have an accurate guide to which items sell fastest.

The amount of stock needed will depend on the type of fair you are going to. It goes without saying that you will generally need far less stock with you for a small school fair than for a large, two or three day event. You will probably need a different choice of items – more of the smaller pocket money items for the children to buy with a selection of your larger more expensive designs to show the staff and parents what you can do, and hopefully to make some more profitable sales.

If you are booking large, expensive craft fairs make sure that you have far more stock than you think you will need. Thousands or even tens of thousands of people may pass your stand and although they won't all stop, a percentage of them will. You need to sell a large number of items to make it profitable, so make sure that you have plenty of designs in your undertable stock room so that you can keep replenishing your display as you sell.

After all, if you don't sell them all it just means that you have plenty of stock for the next few weeks and you can take a few days off from making to recover your strength!

## Creating your stock

In general it's much better to build up enough stock to cover you for a number of fairs rather than being on a constant treadmill to make items for each event.

If your craft can be adapted, create some form of assembly line for yourself. It's always quicker to paint all the petals in the flower design – doing twenty or thirty cards at once and then go back to the beginning and paint all the leaves. It will speed up your creation process by a surprising amount and they will still all be handcrafted and just a little bit different from each other.

Most crafts can be adapted like this and it really does make much better use of your time. If you're sewing lots of cushions, repeat one stage for a number of them and then go through the whole batch again doing another stage, continuing like this until you have created your stock of a design.

There's nothing wrong with developing some form of production line for yourself. It doesn't mean that your items are manufactured or mass produced, you are still creating each one by hand but you are using your time as efficiently as you can. Then you can plan your schedule and give yourself the time you need to create new designs and new ideas for your business.

## New designs.

You should introduce new items regularly otherwise your regular customers will get bored and stop looking at your stall – more importantly, they will stop buying!

Every designer creates new collections. Try to follow the idea of the big fashion houses and have Spring and Summer collections and Winter or Christmas collections.

Not only will you be able to introduce new items to your customers, it will keep your mind fresh as well and give you a timetable to work to.

You can still keep your overall image, but adapt it to the seasons or special events. You can also follow the fashion house more closely and work with the colours of the season, keeping your brand fresh and up to date.

## Following fashion

Trends are a great boost for crafters. You can develop a new item or a new design quickly when you see a new fashion and have it available for sale within days or certainly weeks.

A good example of this was the sudden popularity of e-book readers and then tablets. Savvy crafters who worked in fabrics and leather developed quirky, elegant and unique covers and cases for these new must haves. Perfect Christmas presents to go with the main present – an e-book reader! You can even personalise them in some crafts.

You can also keep your designs up to date by working in the latest colour palettes and keeping up to date with styles and trends. It will make your designs relevant and modern.

Being out of date can be the death knell to a small business. Traditional designs will almost always be in demand, but 'vintage ' will fall out of fashion as quickly as it appeared. Nowhere – everywhere – nowhere!

But there is a downside to following fashion.

When an item becomes fashionable – such as charm bracelets for instance – there is a window of opportunity but then everyone jumps on the bandwagon and begins to sell them. You'll see charms everywhere from the big department stores, jewellery shops, fashion stores, gift stores and local markets. You'll also see them on a number of other craft stalls. At that point you're just one of hundreds of places that are selling charms and your sales will inevitably fall. Worse still, most fashions are quite short lived and when they've gone out of fashion you could be left with items you'll never sell.

So when you are creating a design that is right 'on trend' you have to take a different approach to your stock control. You can certainly start out by trying a few designs to see if they will work. Then make as many as you can so that you can catch the trend. Then as soon as you see the trend appearing everywhere – slow down in your making process because your sales will probably begin to tail off and then stop all together as it becomes last years fashion. The big stores have sales and outlet stores to get rid of their excess old stock, you should just try to avoid having excess unwanted stock.

The trick is to be the leader, not one of the many followers. Once something is the very height of fashion and seen everywhere - it's too late.

## Storing your stock

It depends on your craft, but some finished items can take up a lot of room!

You have to take this into account when you are creating your business in the first place. If you make wooden pens you can keep hundreds or even thousands on shelves in the spare bedroom, but if you make hand carved tables you are going to need more storage room although probably not as much stock.

Whatever your craft and product range, once you've made your creations you must keep them in good condition. They have to be clean and well presented, a customer won't choose a card that's bent on the corner, a cushion cover that's dusty or a piece of silver that's tarnished. Worse still, that one item that's slightly soiled or damaged will damage the image of your entire display and your reputation as a quality craft worker.

Work out how to keep your stock in premium condition and store it properly so that you can have as long as shelf life as possible. You can find a very good range of shelving and plastic boxes that won't cost you a fortune and you'll find that it's a very good investment in the long run. You'll save time and money because you will be able to keep your items in pristine condition and you'll be able to find what you've made!

Personally I prefer to keep stock – both parts and completed items – in a range of clear plastic boxes with secure lids. This keeps everything clean, fresh, neat and visible. Cardboard boxes soon get dusty and damaged.

Some crafts can also be packed individually in clear bags that can double as your presentation packaging. The polypropylene bags that you pack your handmade cards in look professional as well as keeping our valuable work clean and in top condition.

You can also package some other crafts such as knitting, fabric work, photography or handmade soaps.

You might want to have some pieces open on your display, but you can keep most of your stock packed and protected, which will save you time and money in the long run and will make you look more professional and will therefore add value to your designs.

## Buying in Bulk.

Planning and making your stock in advance means you can buy your materials in bulk.

There can be an enormous difference between wholesale and retail prices and any money that you manage to save from your costs can either make you more competitive or adds directly to your profits.

Look in the craft magazines or on-line to find suppliers. Depending on your craft, you might also be able to find some wholesale companies close to home, but don't be afraid to look further afield. I source my raw materials from all over the world and it's far easier now with the internet than it used to be years ago.

You do have to prove that you are in business before you can deal with most wholesalers, and you also have to be prepared to purchase more stock at one time than if you were simply going to a shop. But as well as saving money you may also be able to find unusual raw materials for your work and see items in their catalogues or warehouses that you hadn't even thought of, giving you an advantage over those who stick close to home when buying their parts.

When you are buying in bulk it can sometimes be worthwhile to take a close look at your designs to decide which components you can standardise rather than having a small quantity of many different parts doing basically the same thing.

Obviously you want to keep variety in your designs but there are normally some areas where you can standardise. Use a standard ear fitting rather than four or five different styles. Make your cards in two or three sizes so that you can buy that size card and bag in greater numbers rather than making lots of different shapes and sizes – it will make storage easier as well.

If you paint ceramics choose one or two basic mugs to work with rather than different shapes and sizes – it will create a style throughout your work as well as making it easier to source and store your stock.

The same process can be used for almost any craft. It doesn't limit your creativity or make your designs boring, infact it makes the designs more important because your customer isn't distracted by all the different shapes and sizes, you can create a 'look' that makes it easier on the eye. It also makes it easier to create sets or a collection because your designs will automatically work together.

You'll also have to have a source of packaging – paper bags, carrier bags, bubble wrap, boxes or tissue paper – depending on your craft. Try to find a wholesale supplier for these items as well. Other crafters that you are working with should be able to direct you to local suppliers.

# How to Promote yourself

Promoting your new craft business can take a number of different forms.

The Oxford English dictionary defines 'promotion' as an activity that supports or encourages a venture and the publicising of a product or venture, so as to increase sales or public awareness.

Many people think of a promotion as being simply discounting prices, and while that is a valid method of attracting more customers, promoting your business can and should take many more forms than simply relying on price.

## Price promotions

We are surrounded by all sorts of promotions nowadays in the retail world.

BOGOF's
50% discount.
Three-for-two
even 70% off!
January sale.
Christmas event

They can all sound very tempting, and some of them even work, attracting us to buy things we didn't really want and certainly didn't intend to buy. But we have become quite jaded as consumers, simply not believing most of these promises. The half price sale finishes on Sunday and 50% off sale starts on Monday!

But that doesn't mean that you should completely forget about developing your own promotions and special offers, you just have to be a bit more imaginative with them.

## Bundled discounts

This is the type of marketing policy that covers things like the BOGOF that you find at supermarkets, but it doesn't have to be that obvious.

Clearly, if you're going to offer Buy One Get One Free, the price of each one has to cover the costs of two. You are not in the business of giving your work away. Even if you are raising money for a charity – you're still supposed to be raising money.

You might decide that your marketing policy is to offer bargains, to be the discount outlet of the craft fair, in which case you've probably gone for bright, primary colours in your design and the image of your stand and basic packaging. If this is your brand style – and it is a perfectly legitimate one - you will want to make a show of your discount offers because this will be your main selling point.

But if your style is dainty gemstone jewellery or unique pieces of handmade glass ornaments, you don't really want your elegant craft stall to look like a pile them high supermarket or a £1 store. In this case you can still introduce the idea of bundled discounts in a more subtle way.

For instance, if you sell a necklace and a pair of earrings that match, but you normally sell them separately, you can have a discount or special price for buying the set.

If you sell handpainted mugs, you could have an offer where a customer who purchases three can pick a fourth one free.

Look at your own range and see how you could create packages. 5 for 4 on handcrafted cards, free curtain tiebacks with curtains. There are endless ways of offering discounts to attract a customer to buy more than just a single piece. You just have to be a little bit imaginative about it.

## Time specific discounts.

You could have a 'special show price' on a particular type of item. You can set a discount 'just for this event.'

You see this kind of promotion quite regularly at large events, normally offered by the large, professional companies that travel the country selling at flower shows, County shows, horse shows and the like.

If you buy from them on the day, you pay a special show price. If you purchase later from their website, the item will cost you more.

The whole idea of this is to make people part with their money there and then, rather than picking up a leaflet, going away and thinking about it. It's a style of promotion that is quite often used for more expensive products, where people are more likely to go away and think about it rather than making an impulse purchase, but it can work on any type of product. The idea is to make people buy it now, because more often than not once they've left your stall you have lost a sale. People might genuinely intend to check your website later but life takes over!

## Free gifts

Everyone loves something free.

Free is a magic word in marketing.

Free will stop almost anyone in their tracks and make them look.

So how can you use this marketing idea in your business?

Some people literally give something away free. For instance, they have a bowl of boiled sweets on the counter with the idea that this will make people stop and take a sweet. Of course they will stop and take a sweet and some of them might even look at your craft while doing it – others might just be putting off buying lunch at your expense!

I prefer to make people work for their free gift or more to the point - buy something!

The best way of using the free gift marketing method is to encourage people to buy more. Spend over £20 and receive a free jewelled hair clip. Spend over £50 on hand quilted cushion covers and receive free cushion inserts. Spend over £10 and receive a free gift box.

The exact details, the exact levels of spend, and the free gift is entirely up to you. It will depend on your style and your craft, and it will depend on the type of customer you're aiming at. It will also depend on your profit margins.

## Sale time

The problem with the word Sale is that it has been overused and has lost its power to attract. Some shops constantly have sales and people stop looking.

But it can still be worth using.

If you have some stock that just isn't selling it can be worth bundling together and putting the word sale on it.

But I would normally try various other methods first.

Altering the prices - up as well as down.

Sometimes an item that is not selling will suddenly become a bestseller when you put the price up! Strange but true – a lot of people judge items by the price, if it's too cheap it mustn't be worth having!

A bargain basket can be a very good way of selling designs that you want to reduce in price.

There's something about a bargain basket or box that just attracts people! They love rooting through looking for a bargain. Of course you have to make sure that your items are not just going to end up in a tangled, ruined mess at the end of the day.

How you manage this problem will depend on what you make and what designs you use in the first place. You might have to package them individually or put them in clear bags.

It's also worth limiting the number of items you put in your bargain basket – people feel a more urgent need to buy if there are only a few left!

## Product promotion.

Although price promotions are fine to use at one time or another, you should have promotions that are a continual part of your business plan.

You should always promote your business.

These types of promotions are designed to encourage customer loyalty, create the style of your brand, to remind potential customers about you and of course to increase sales.

Make sure that everyone who has a piece of your work knows that it is your unique craft and design. Some events, especially charity events, ask you to provide a gift for their raffle -and of course you want to support the charity - but make sure that whoever wins your piece knows where it's from. There's nothing wrong with supporting your business as well as the charity.

When a customer buys a piece from, you make sure that they have the details of where they can find you and how they can contact you so that they can make future purchases. When someone receives some of your handcrafted pieces as a gift, make sure they know that you are the designer and how they can purchase more for their collection.

Every piece of work that leaves your stall should be branded in some way. The way you add your logo will depend on the style of your craft but don't think that it has to be something expensively produced by a professional printer. The beauty of your craft is that it is individually handmade, so there's nothing wrong with your packaging being handmade as well. In fact it adds to your overall style.

If you make chunky vintage style jewellery, why not find some manila luggage tags and write your details by hand on them. If your work is in delicate handpainted silk, create a delicate leaflet to put in the box with it.

Again, learn from the experts. Visit the stores and actually 'look' at the packaging. It's very easy to take things for granted. We're so used to being surrounded by products that sometimes we don't really look anymore.

Have a proper look at the products on offer in your range – whether that's jewellery, handmade quilts, ceramics, woodwork, home decor – whatever you feel is in the same type of product range. Then look at the different styles and price ranges. They will all be presented in different ways – but they'll all have the makers details on them somewhere.

Find a style you like and that you feel will complement your designs and work from there to create your own unique packaging and labelling.

## Talking about your craft.

One of the nice things about selling face-to-face is the fact that you actually get a chance to meet your customers. So make the most of it.

If you sell jewellery you have to be aware that they could buy a piece of jewellery anywhere - at any of the other stalls at the fair, at any fashion shop, jewellery shop or even supermarket. But they want to buy the jewellery from you. So talk to them about it.

The same is true whatever your craft, handmade cards and papercraft or large pieces of handcarved wooden furniture. Your pieces are unique to you and you should make sure that your customers know that they are talking to a craft worker who loves their work. Even at a craft fair some customers don't seem to realise that you actually make everything you offer for sale.

When you look around at many events, you will always find some designers who just sit behind their stall, often reading a book. Put yourself in the position of the potential customer. If you were thinking of buying something from that stall, you'd probably just walk past. Why should you show interest in their work if they can't show interest in you?

You also have to remember that a lot of people would feel uncomfortable about disturbing someone who has obviously got something better to do than to talk to them.

So, stand behind or to the side of your stall. Smile at people, engage with them, say hello.

You don't have to pounce on every potential customer, that is counter-productive, but you should show them that you are aware that they are standing in front of your stall and that you are willing to talk to them if they would like to ask a question.

When you do open a conversation, talk about your craft. What makes it different? What is your USP (unique selling point). After all, you now know what your style is, so you should also know why your designs are different to anyone else's.

Do you always include a piece of Jade in your jewellery designs, because it is the gem of health, wealth and long life?

Are your designs made from pieces of polished glass that you personally collect from the beach?

Is recycling an important aspect of your work?

Can you personalise any of the items on your stand while that wait?

What led you into your craft, what is your story?

Tell them that you can customise pieces, changing the colours of the fabrics, altering the length of a bracelet or personalising your design. Taking orders for bespoke pieces can be a very valuable addition to your new business.

When somebody does buy a piece, point out - without pressure – other items in your range that are designed to make a set.

And don't be afraid to talk to someone, even though you have a strong feeling that they are not going to buy anything from you, at least today. They may well come back on another day when they do want to buy a piece, and they will remember that you were friendly and didn't pressurise them.

Or you might sell to the people who were listening to your conversation - lots of people prefer to join a crowd when they wouldn't approach you themselves.

It also creates a good impression if anyone is looking around for craft workers to take a stall at their event or give a talk to their group. They will be looking for people who are open and approachable.

## Demonstrating your craft.

This might sound a bit odd, showing other people how to compete with you! But in fact, showing people how you make your craft can be a very good way of selling to them.

It can work in two different ways.

You can create starter packs, so that you can teach people how to create their own designs.

Next time you're at a large craft shop, look around at how many products are being sold to crafters. The range of kits is huge and just seems to grow each time I visit. There's nothing to stop you put in your own product range together and selling these starter packs to your students and possibly at craft fairs, through your local craft shop on on-line.

You should also have some of your own handmade designs with you when you demonstrate. People who are interested in learning a new craft are interested in handcrafted items. And while they will enjoy making their own, they are beginners, and your designs will be much more professional. So don't be surprised when you sell some of the samples you've taken with you. In fact, that should be part of your plan! Also make sure that you take plenty of promotional literature. You want them to be able to find you when they decide they want to buy a piece from you.

You can do these demonstrations to a number of different groups. Some libraries have regular events for people to learn new skills. You might find that you can work with the girl guides or brownies or as entertainment at birthday parties. You could offer your skills to women's groups or maybe even set up a package and offer it for hen parties. Learn to think outside the box.

## Seasonal promotions

There are certain times of the year that are just made for special and unusual gifts.

The shops are experts at providing a product for a season, whether it's Christmas, Easter, the summer holidays, Mother's Day, Father's Day, Royal events, special anniversaries.

There are also some other dates that you might want to add to your list.

Halloween is getting more and more popular, and there are plenty of people who to go to town on their Halloween parties and designs.

And of course don't forget the end of the school year. This can give you two separate opportunities, gifts for teachers and graduation gifts. Even returning to school can create opportunities for special pencil cases, pouches for iPads and tablets, bookmarks, pens or book stickers.

Which of these events you decide to use for your promotions will depend on the type of craft that you design, and how and where you sell it. You will probably be able to think of some more events that would be perfect for your brand.

And there are other special events as well. Weddings, birthdays, new babies, new houses, new jobs - the list can go on and on.

You should always try to follow the lead of the experts, they have spent millions in market research and you can learn from them by just investing a little time and thought.

Seasonal marketing is very important in most types of retail business, whether offering special menus for Christmas parties, Easter eggs, hearts and flowers for Valentine's day or bouquets for Mothers Day.

Never underestimate the call for special gifts.

Everyone has some way of adapting their craft for Christmas gifts – and Christmas shopping begins in earnest in September or October, December is far too late. You should be preparing Christmas stock in the summer if you want to have enough, because by October and November you will be too busy actually selling your product at craft fairs. It is very important to capitalise on this season. The sales you make at this peak period will support you in the quieter season until fairs begin again in earnest in the spring.

But Christmas is not the only opportunity for creating seasonal designs. And unlike Christmas, most people do the their shopping much closer to the date for Valentines Day, Easter, Mother's and Father's Day, so it's worth having something suitable on your stand when you're at fairs around those dates.

Take some time to think about the other events that people want to remember with a special gift –

The birth of a new baby, or a Christening.

Engagements and weddings,

special birthdays,

passing exams,

moving home,

a promotion or retirement.

You don't want to categorise all your products, it would restrict your ability to sell rather than enhancing it, but you should certainly consider at least some of these events when creating your design range

## The Christmas season

The Christmas season is arguably the most important part of the year for your new craft business.

The Christmas season is important for all retailers and for some it is literally make or break. Bad Christmas sales can mean that a big high street name disappears early in January or February.

So if it's that important for huge high street brands, it should be important for you too. You don't have to focus all your hopes on the Christmas season – after all you don't want your business to disappear in January – but you should certainly aim to make as much as you can in this important part of the year.

It's that time of the year when you will find the most events, and some of the biggest events. The season runs from mid September to about the middle of December. The main out-of-town Christmas fairs are completed by the end of November or the very beginning of December and then events such as Christmas markets will run almost up to the holiday itself.

Some crafters spend most of the year preparing for the Christmas season, and for any crafter it can be the most hectic time of the year - in fact, it's best if you get your own Christmas family preparations done before September!

So make sure that you have your Christmas gifts available in plenty of time for Christmas shoppers. December is too late for all but the last minute item and shoppers that leave their gift shopping until the last few days are going to be panicking at a shopping mall not visiting your craft fair. The exception to this is when you have a stall at an event in the middle of town or a mall, such as a Christmas Market, then you do have the opportunity to catch the last minute shopper looking for something different – and that can be very profitable!

But as a general guide, most of your customers will begin to look seriously at planning their gift list by the time you have your craft fairs and events in September.

The end of the school summer holidays seems to trigger thoughts of Christmas shopping for a lot of people, so you need to have your potential gifts available for them at that time and you need to start planning, designing and making long before that.

The big high street stores start planning for the next Christmas just after the January sales!

And it's not only the fact that you might want to produce some Christmas designs – the actual type of purchasing changes as it gets towards the vital Christmas season.

During the rest of the year, your customer might be looking for a special birthday present, a new baby gift, a wedding, engagement of anniversary present or a treat for herself – but whichever it is, it's probably a single gift, which means that she can spend all her money on fewer items. Maybe some gifts to take home from a holiday, maybe there are a couple of birthdays in the month. But in my experience, it is easier to sell more expensive, individual pieces during the main part of the year.

Once it comes to September, customers are thinking of Christmas gifts. Gifts plural, so each one has to be more considered. Some will still be large gifts – large in value, not necessarily size – but many will be smaller, lower priced presents. Gifts for school teachers, neighbours, people at work, Secret Santas, small gifts for friends and family. Many of these will have a set price point and your customer will be looking for something that is different but that still falls into this previously decided price bracket.

You should take this into account when you're designing your Christmas stock. They don't have to be obviously Christmas designs, in fact you should only make a proportion of your pieces with overtly seasonal designs – not everyone wants to buy everything covered in snowmen and reindeer!

Your customers will have a price point in mind as they look for each gift and you should hit these prices in your display. £5, £10, £15, £20 (or $'s). Check the displays of gifts in your local department stores to see how they do this.

You could decide to take an even bigger piece of marketing from the department stores and use some of their promotional marketing techniques.

'Three for Two.'

'£5 each – 5 for £20.'

'£6 each - Two for £10'

The most popular offer is '3 for 2' - of course remember that it's always the lowest priced item that is free!

This is another time you should learn from the experts.

They have found that, particularly at Christmas, this promotion will encourage people to buy two items, in order to get the third one free, rather than just the one item that they actually went in for. In fact, you can find yourself spending longer in front of the shelves wondering who you will give the extra two gifts to and what you should choose, when it would be much quicker and cheaper to just pick the one you wanted in the first place. But that's the point. It works. So if the big stores can make the most of it - so can you.

Of course, do remember that they are all priced to cover the cost of the three items, even though as a shopper you feel that you are getting a bargain, and there's that wonderful magic word again – FREE!

So if you decide to use this promotion, do make sure that you work out your prices correctly. You're not actually in the business of giving away your designs – even at Christmas!

Your customers can find the perfect gift for almost anybody and it will be unique. Whoever they give it to won't be able to go to the January sales and see how much they spent! And they don't have to worry about someone else giving exactly the same gift - a problem you do have to consider when you choose a book or DVD!

All styles of craft can be adapted for the Christmas gift market.

If you focus on fashion jewellery and fun and funky designs then Christmas tree bauble earrings and bright red and green bangles might be the way you decide to go.

You can adapt many crafts for the Christmas season. Hand painted china with snowmen on them, baby bibs sporting elves and reindeer, candle holders in festive shades, table runners covered in beautiful snowflakes and of course, beautiful Christmas cards and tree decorations. But do remember, any that are unsold on Christmas Eve either have to be given as your own Christmas gifts or packed away for next year.

On the other hand, you may prefer to simply make more of your normal designs and package them beautifully so that they are a gift that somebody can simply purchase and give, already boxed and ready to be presented, especially if you add a gift bag. Many of the Gift Boxes in the department stores actually contain very ordinary products, they are just presented very well. It can make a surprising difference to the way your customer reacts to your designs if you simply present it in a gift bag. They don't have to think any further about that present – it's gift wrapped – job done. You've saved them time as well as the extra cost of gift wrapping.

The seasonal promotion doesn't just have to stop with your actually craft and how you package it.

You can – and should - carry the idea through to your entire shopfront.

Again, take a leaf out of the expert's book. The department stores spend thousands of pounds decorating their windows. The shopping centres make a big feature of their Christmas decorations, and town centres make an entire event out of turning on the Christmas lights. They do this because it attracts customers, and it puts them in the Christmas mood, which makes them think of buying presents and spending money.

So join in.

Decorate your table. Use tinsel or fairy lights along the front. Maybe you have enough room for a miniature Christmas tree or some snowflakes and if the style is right for your image you could even wear a Santa hat.

Whatever you decide, make your stall festive, encourage people to think of buying Christmas gifts when they see your display. Although serious Christmas shopping starts in September, it's normally better to wait until the beginning of November before you pull out all the stops in your Christmas display but it is effective. When potential customers see your stall looking like a Christmas display they will subconsciously think Christmas. Some organisers are very good about creating the right atmosphere and so are some crafters, but a surprising number are not and if that is the case, your stand will really stand out at the fair and will at least create the right atmosphere around you and your products.

Carry the theme through your whole display. If you have decided to use beautiful gift boxes as part of your promotion, display them on your table, make them look like a wonderful display of presents. Don't hide them away with the idea that customers should know you'll package the gift for them.

Think how the stores display all the beautiful gift wrapped boxes that they have on offer at this time of the year. Very often the products inside them are nothing special. Body lotions, shower gels, hand creams, maybe a china mug with some sweets inside it, maybe a tie and some cufflinks. Many of these wonderful looking gift boxes contain quite ordinary products, but they are packaged in a beautiful way in beautiful boxes with ribbon around them. It's easy to just buy them, take them home and put them under the tree.

People are always short of time, especially at Christmas time, and buying this type of ready to give gifts is so much easier to do. It takes the thinking and the work out of the process, so customers are attracted to anything that will save them time and make life easy.

Yes, it would be cheaper to buy a nice box and all the body lotions and package them yourself, but people don't do that, they pay extra to have it done for them.

So when they see your designs beautifully packaged and presented, it will automatically look more like a gift and that's the effect you want.

When you're selling at the Christmas season it's all about getting the sales.

People want to buy gifts.

They will part with their money.

They have to go home with all the presents they need - the stocking fillers, small gifts for friends and neighbours, the gifts for teachers and for work colleagues as well as great aunt Sally and mother's next door neighbour.

They have to find these gifts on the list and they will spend their money somewhere. Your main aim at this time of the year is to get them to spend it with you.

That is why you invest money in taking a stand at the fair in the first place, so invest a little more in creating beautiful packaging.

## The other side of Christmas

And no – I don't mean the January sales!

The problem with Christmas is that the shops are full of Christmas stuff!

That's wonderful if you're looking for Christmas presents, cards and decorations but an absolute nightmare if you're looking for cards and presents for birthdays, anniversaries or any other event that's not Christmas. And I say this as someone who has a number of family birthdays and anniversaries that fall in the October – January slot.

There are many opportunities to profit from this gap in the market. For instance, if you sell handmade cards you are in an ideal situation to solve this problem for your customers. The card shops are stuffed full of Christmas cards from about September, with all other events crushed into a corner at the back of the shop, so if you want a card for a birthday in December you have to either be really well organised and buy it in July or make do with the tiny choice you have in December.

It can be so tempting to pack your stall with every imaginable design of Christmas card, but don't. You can certainly have a selection of beautiful, exclusive Christmas card designs, but you're never going to be able to compete with the millions of cards on sale in every store and from every charity you can think of.

But if you have a good selection of birthday, anniversary, good luck, congratulation, new baby, new house, wedding, engagement, sympathy, and cards for every other event you can think of you will be able to fill the huge gap left by everyone else.

And it doesn't finish at Christmas. Any time of the year that is dominated by a special holiday can make it difficult to buy anything not directly associated with that holiday. Valentine's Day, Mother's Day, Easter and Halloween will see the stores swamped with seasonal designs. So although they are a good source of seasonal sales, don't forget the potential customers who are looking for something else.

You should also take this into account when you are creating your beautifully packaged gift boxes. Make some of them more general rather than all Christmas. When a customer is looking for a gift for a birthday in December, they don't want it to look like a Christmas present, they want a birthday present.

The job of any retailer is to supply what the customer wants.

# Recording your progress

So far we have been looking at the actual process of selling.

Designing your craft, pricing it, finding fairs, how to set up your stall and display and sell your designs, how to make the most of seasonal events and where else to look for outlets for your business.

But you also have to remember that you are running a business and you have to learn to be businesslike in how you go about your work.

One of the most important parts of any business is learning how to be methodical and accurate in how you record everything about your business and keeping everything on the right side of the law.

## Keeping Score

It's very important to know exactly how your business is progressing. Keeping records might seem boring and unnecessary and most people prefer to avoid the paperwork, but it's vital.

First of all you need to keep accurate records of your stock.

Before you go into a fair make an accurate list of the stock you are taking and re-check it at the end of the day. *Do this every time.* It may seem like an unnecessary burden but it is the only way you will be able to accurately tell how your business is doing.

The detail you will go into depends on your product, but it needs to give you enough information to enable you to make judgements of what items are selling, which are most profitable and which you should concentrate on for the future.

Over a number of fairs you may also be able to see some pattern emerging, which means that you can tailor your stock to a specific market - type of fair, geographical area, time of year. You might find that the type of design or price range that you sell in one type of venue is dramatically different from another type of venue. It's tempting to think that you'll be able to remember, or you'll get a 'feel' for the type of stock you should take, but you'll be wrong. Once you actually look at the figures it can be quite a surprise to see what actually are your best sellers.

Keeping accurate records of each fair will also enable you to judge what effect a change of price has on your overall performance.

An increase in price may lower your actual sales but increase your profit. Then again, a lowering of your price may increase sales to such an extent that it also increases your profit. And of course there's always the confusing situation where an increase in price leads to an increase in sales.

You can only tell what will happen by trial and error and keeping accurate records so that you can actually plot what is happening from event to event. And selling at craft fairs is the ideal format for making such experiments.

It's much easier to make changes in your prices as you work through different events and places rather than in a shop with the same customers each week. But you can only learn and profit from these valuable lessons if you keep accurate records.

## The Business of Business

This book is mainly about marketing and selling your handmade craft, it is not intended to be a detailed guide to the legal, financial and tax requirements of running a business – any business of any size.

## Find some expert advice

There are many books and courses and websites available where you can find out about these other areas of running your business and I recommend that you invest some time and money in this information so that you can avoid any pitfalls and problems in the future. But the following pages are designed to be an introduction to the areas you will have to consider.

## Legal Requirements

First of all – records. You are of course in business, no matter how small your business is to start with.

Exactly how you choose to set up your business depends on your own circumstances and the size of company you intend to aim for.

There are many sources of information on setting up business - hundreds of books, packages from banks, guides from Local Enterprise Boards and leaflets from the Tax Office.

Study as many of them as you can, so that you understand what will be required of you.

## Forms of Business Organisation

In the UK, the law permits a range of business organisation types, from the sole trader or one man (or woman) unincorporated business at one end of the spectrum, to the massive public limited company at the other. Basically, there are three forms of business organisation available to those setting up an operation:

Sole Trader
Partnership
Limited Company

**Sole Trader**

A Sole Trader is literally what the name suggests.
 One person setting up in business alone.

That person can set up in business without any formalities. All profits are deemed to belong to that person and are taxed as such, and any losses and debts are also the personal responsibility of that one person.

*"A Sole Trader is any one person trading with a view to making a profit"*

A Sole Trader can use his or her own name for the business or choose a trading name.

**Advantages –**

There are no formalities for setting up the business, you can just set it up on day one.

All the profits you make over the year belong to you - so do all the losses!

You have sole control of the business – no one else is going to dictate what you can do.

You can also close down without any formalities if you want to.

**Disadvantages –**

You may be short of start up money.

You have to provide all the management expertise

You are personally responsible for all the debts

**Partnership**

A Partnership is a coming together of two or more people to carry on business with a view to profit. It is created by agreement and partnership articles may be drawn up. It grew from the law of contract and the principals of agency as developed by the courts. During the latter part of the nineteenth century, partnership law was codified by the enactment of the Partnership Act 1890.

The definition of partnership in the Act is:

*"the relationship which subsists between persons carrying on a business in common with a view to profit."*

The law states that not more than twenty people can be in partnership, except for professional partnerships. (Lawyers, accountants etc)

You would be setting up a partnership if you decide to go into business with a friend or member of your family rather than they just working for your business..

**Advantages –**

You can raise more capital

The pressures of running a business are shared

The legal requirements for forming a partnership are very few. The 1890 Act just regulates what happens if partners have not agreed.

Profits and losses are shared.

**Disadvantages –**

You don't have sole control of the business

You are jointly and separately responsible for the debts (this can be a significant disadvantage if someone disappears!)

There can be problems if the partners disagree and cannot work their way through the differences.

**Limited Company**

In English Law, a Limited Company is a separate entity artificially created. It can sue, be sued, be prosecuted and fined.

It is separate to the shareholders and the Shareholders liability is limited to their shareholding (the amount invested)

A Limited Liability Company can be defined as a legal person, separate from the owners.

If you are at the beginning of a craft business that you plan to grow and that requires larger amounts of capital investment in equipment and premises, such as a ceramics or glass company or creating homemade food or preserves, you may want to consider setting up as a limited company from the start.

**Advantages –**

Limited liability to the amount of the shareholding – so your potential losses are limited, although in practice you will normally have to sign personal guarantees if you want to obtain a large loan from the bank.

In theory it is easier to raise large sums of capital.

Companies can be professionally managed by directors.

Shares can be sold – even floated on the stock exchange if your company is large enough.

**Disadvantages –**

A Limited company is expensive to start (lawyers and accountants have to form it)

You have to file official accounts, which will normally involve working with accountants.

In the USA there are similar structures, the Sole Proprietorship, Partnerships, the LLC (Limited Liability Company) and the Corporation. You should check your local business requirements and take the relevant professional advice.

## What does this mean for you?

Most craft businesses that will be trading at craft fairs in the UK or USA will be either a 'sole trader' or a 'partnership'. Either type of firm can employ other people.

If you intend to work on your own, or to employ others but to be 'the boss' you will be operating as a sole trader - supplying all of the capital, earning all of the profits and being responsible for any losses. This is the easiest way to set up.

However, if you are setting up business with a friend or relative and sharing the financial input, financial responsibility and the decision making, you will be setting up a `partnership'. You will share the costs and the profits or losses. At this stage, no matter how good your friendship, you should set out some form of partnership agreement. In fact, an agreement can help to separate your friendship from your business relationship and it can reduce disagreements if all matters such as work load, responsibilities and the amount of investment in time and money are all discussed at the very start rather than just left as `understandings'!

## The Tax Office

Once you become self employed or earn a second income you have to take responsibility for your tax position and your National Insurance. You will have to fill in a self-assessment tax form at the end of each financial year and file it on time to avoid statutory fines.

Your local tax office will give you all the information you need, and you can also find plenty of help online from official sites, but basically you must keep records of all your income and all your business expenses. That is whatever money comes in from customers and whatever money you spend in order to carry on the business.

In the USA you should contact the IRS and check their website.

Wherever you are setting up a business, the most important thing to remember is that you are in business – even just doing a few craft events a year is a small business and you will have to notify the relevant tax office, even if your income is below the tax threshold. It's much better to be upfront from the start, rather than to risk getting your taxes in a mess later.

So, keep receipts and details of all that you spend for your business and all the money you take when you make sales. The easiest way to keep the records is to file and record all the receipts or invoices you receive for money you spend and record all the money you take at each craft fair or that you earn from special contracts.

There are many books and websites on bookkeeping and accounting for small business – this isn't meant to be one of them! But the basic rules are – record everything!

Profit is not the amount of money you come away with on the day, or the amount of money you take overall. Profit is the difference between how much you take from customers and how much it costs you to do that.

So, keep an accurate record of all the money you take in – whether that is in cash or cheque and credit card payments – record every sale. This is your income.

Also record everything you spend to run your business – you have to have proof of this, so keep all your receipts and invoices safety filed, you will need them for your accounts and your tax return. If you spend £20 on paper for making your cards, paint for your art or thread for your sewing projects and don't get a receipt – you have just thrown that £20 away – you can't set it against your profits.

You can claim costs that you have legitimately incurred for running your business. So you can list the parts you use to create your products - obviously.

But if you need a new pair of scissors for your work, or you need to have business cards printed, or you choose to have a mobile phone that you only use for business, or the travelling expenses to get to and from the fair and the rent you pay to the organiser for your stand. The packaging material that you use when you sell your product, the cloth and display stands that you bought and the cash box to put your takings in are all legitimate costs. So is a college or correspondence course that you have done to help you run your business, storage boxes and shelving that you use just for your business, or accounting or design software – all of these items and more are legitimate expenses and can be listed in your accounts.

But while creativity is important in most of your business - don't get too creative in the accounting part of it. Buying some new designs while you're away does not mean that you can claim your holiday as a business trip!

## VAT

The other type of tax that is involved in business is VAT – or Value Added Tax.

All of us pay VAT on things we buy but you don't normally notice it because it's included in the price on the label. Once you start buying wholesale the prices in the catalogues, on the website or in the warehouse will be plus VAT (which is 20% at the time of writing) and this can add quite a lot to your final invoice if you don't take it into account at the time.

As a business you can register for VAT and once your turnover of taxable goods and services reaches £79,000 you have to register for VAT.

Once you are registered for VAT you have to charge VAT on your products and you can reclaim the VAT you have paid on goods and services for your business.

Some items are zero rated – such as books (not e-books) baby wear and children's clothes, cakes and biscuits (although there are some very strange exceptions. Chocolate chip cookies are zero rated, but chocolate covered biscuits are standard rate).

If you are selling items that fall into this range it can be worthwhile registering voluntarily for VAT because in selling zero-rated items and buying standard rated items you would be able to receive a refund from HMRC (HM Revenue and Customs). You will have to submit regular VAT returns and there are statutory fines for being late in submitting them, so even if you are able to receive regular refunds on the VAT you have spent as a business you do have to put some work in for it.

The HMRC website (www.hmrc.gov.uk) has very detailed information about VAT as well as lots of information about starting a business, keeping records, tax and national insurance. It's worth spending some time reading through it.

In America the IRS (www.irs.gov/Businesses) also provides a great deal of useful information for setting up a business.

## Other legal requirements

Once you are in business it is also your personal responsibility to comply with all legal requirements.

Each industry has different requirements and it is up to you to research the industry that you are entering because ignorance of the law is no defence if you do run into problems.

For instance if you are going to be making jams and chutneys it is vital that you comply with all the labelling requirements listing ingredients, best before dates, your name and address and a number of other legal requirements. You would also need to comply with the food safety legislation. All of this legislation applies to you just as much as it does to a huge factory and although you may well 'get away with it' – you shouldn't even try! You are producing a food stuff that others will be eating and for your own safety as well as everyone else's you need to comply with the regulations.

If you are making wooden toys for children you have to comply with toy safety regulations and if you are making jewellery you have to follow the legal regulations for hallmarking precious metals and the regulations on nickel content.

Every area of business has its own rules and regulations and the best time to find out what they are is at the very beginning rather than when you find you've fallen foul of the law. There is a wealth of information available online and many specialist wholesale companies will also include information about legal requirements on their website.

## Insurance

You might think that you have good insurance cover, but your car insurance and building and contents insurance are not normally designed for business and might specifically exclude business use – so do check. It will be far too late to find out once you have to make a claim. Your insurance company could refuse to pay out even if your claim has nothing to do with your business.

It's also important to protect yourself by ensuring that you have the correct product and public liability insurance as well as general business insurance.

Organisers will insist that you have insurance cover before they accept your booking, but you should have insurance anyway for your own safety. If you are a member of the National Market Traders Federation, your membership includes insurance and there are some insurance brokers who specialise in cover for craft workers, a web search will bring up a current list of companies who offer specialist insurance. You should also be able to arrange cover if you are a member of a craft guild or association and fellow crafters will be glad to share information with you if you ask them. We all had to start sometime.

Although you must have liability insurance to be able to make a booking at craft fairs, you might also want to think about other business cover to insure your stock and any loss you might incur if you are unable to work or lose your stock through some disaster. The level of insurance that you might choose will depend on how much you have invested in your business and how large a part it plays in your overall financial picture.

You will also need to alter your car insurance as you will now be using it for trade rather than just personal use. You should also check your home insurance. Many insurers will allow you to cover your computers used for business purposes at home, but some will not cover your home if it is used for business, especially if you have customers visiting you at home – do check.

# Growing your business.

### Where will you go from here

The decisions you make about the way you want your business to go and how you want it to grow are entirely personal.

They will depend on you, your personal circumstances, what you want to put into your business and what you want to get out of it. There is no right or wrong.

I have been in business since the late 1970s (oh, that makes me feel old - I started very young!) And for many years I ran a business with lots of staff, dealing with big multinational companies, and lots of overseas interests, and I loved it.

But things changed when I was diagnosed with M.E. (chronic fatigue syndrome). I had to make some rather drastic changes in my life. Now, I design and make healing crystal jewellery. I mentor small businesses, and give talks to start up groups. I write books on business and alternative therapies, and I run my small family business through craft fairs and events and online websites. I can work from home and set my own timetable, and even though I would never have imagined I would be doing this, I love this lifestyle as well.

When you start your own business, the whole idea is to have more control over your life.

If you are starting your handmade craft business as you leave college or university, you will probably have great plans for creating a brand that you will be able to launch into the mainstream, and that is great. People with great brands that grow from small seeds are the lifeblood of the economy. That is how the great brands start. After all, Marks and Spencer started as a market stall in Leeds and many of our modern designer brands started small at craft fairs.

If this is your plan, the process of selling face-to-face to your customer will allow you to develop your style. You will be able to get feedback about your work and your designs and find out what people really like about it and what type of customer is actually buying your designs and all of this will help you when you want to expand your business.

But equally, there is nothing wrong with keeping your craft business small and under your own control.

There are thousands of people who are making a comfortable living by designing and making handcrafted products that they sell face-to-face to their customers. They have a loyal following and a regular season of events that they do year after year and they have no desire to start employing people and having their own business premises.

And you will find craft workers that fall into the middle. They do have their own premises, maybe a workshop or a retail outlet and a small staff that help them run the business.

There are no rules, you just need to find a way that suits you and your lifestyle.

## Selling online.

Having a presence online can complement selling face-to-face.

When you are talking to people at a craft event you can direct them to your website or some of your other designs on etsy, folksy, eBay or some specialist site. Not all crafts lend themselves to selling on-line, but many do.

If you are not comfortable about sending your items out in the post or by carrier you can still have a website to display your designs and promote the shows you can be found at. If you do have a list of your shows online and work from home, be careful not to display your physical address, you are effectively telling people when you will be away from home!

You can use your blog to keep in contact with your regular customers, or create an e-mail list so that you can keep your customers up to date and let them know about the latest craft events.

If you do party plan you can have a website that you can direct potential customers to, where they can either see your range of handcrafted designs or they can make bookings for a party. You could even add a shop so that they can actually purchase from you on-line.

Social media is a wonderful way of keeping in contact with your customers and promoting your business. It gives the small business a voice .

The type of online presence that you choose will again depend on the style of your business, the type of craft that you create and who your target customer is.

If your style is fun and funky, then social media is probably perfect for you. If you specialise in wedding craft, your target customers will be young women, and again social media is a perfect way of connecting with them and keeping in contact. In fact, wedding craft is one of the areas where you definitely should collect e-mail addresses. When you have someone's wedding date, you can target some promotions to those potential customers at the right time. After all, if you are a jeweller you don't just have to think about the bridal jewellery. There's jewellery for the bridesmaids, cuff links or tiepins for the groom the best man and the ushers.

Other crafts can be adapted as well, for stationary, table decorations, Wedding favours, gifts for the Mother of the Bride and the Mother of the Groom and of course the all important wedding cake.

And of course, do remember that weddings can be a bit like party plan. Orders often lead to more orders as the bridesmaids and guests plan their own weddings. A presence on the web can be invaluable for this type of business.

## The future

Once you've developed your style and have learnt what your customer wants you should have created a healthy and successful business with your handmade craft which will allow you to spend your time doing what you love.

The future direction of your business is entirely up to you, but you should never sit back and think you know it all!

Keep developing your style, keep adapting to changing fashions or trends. Keep your range and image fresh and relevant, it's far too easy to get complacent and stagnate, wondering why people aren't buying from you in the same way anymore.

You might need to find new venues with new customers, you might need to freshen your display or introduce new designs. You need to be able to stand back and see how other people see your designs and your display.

And change is fun!

Part of the joy of creating your own products is learning new skills, working with new products and producing new designs.

So I wish you many years of exciting designing and successful selling.

Printed in Great Britain
by Amazon.co.uk, Ltd.,
Marston Gate.